Deterrence and Reformation

Reviewing the Law on Juvenile Delinquents

Deterrence and Reformation

Reviewing the Law on Juvenile Delinquents

Niharika Goel

Ankit Publications

Delhi - 110009

Deterrence and Reformation: Reviewing the Law on Juvenile Delinquents

First Published in 2022

₹ 695

ISBN 978-81-950132-9-6

Published by : **Ankit Publications**
R-69, 3rd Floor,
Model Town-III, Delhi-110009
Tel. : 09891553405
E-Mail: ankitpublications@gmail.com

Laser Typesetting : Aarati Computers, Delhi-110 009

Printed at : Balaji Offset, Delhi

Contents

Preface 7

1. Introduction 9
2. Reason Behind Separate Treatment of Juveniles 16
3. Doli Incapax and Age of Child : A Dilemma 22
4. Reason Behind Juvenile Delinquency 35
5. Historical Background of the Juvenile Justice System 47
6. Development of Juvenile Justice System in India 55
7. Understanding the Juvenile Justice Act 63
8. Juvenile Justice System versus Criminal Justice System 69
9. Juvenile Perspective Under the International Regime 75
10. Rights of Children Alleged and Found to be in Conflict with the Law 81
11. Objective of the Juvenile Justice Act 113
12. Philosophical Principle Behind Juvenile Homes 122
13. Management of Juvenile Homes 131

14. Special Homes for Juvenile Delinquents 144

15. Place of Safety 159

16. The Concept of Restorative Justice 166

17. The Reality of Juvenile Homes in India:
Hell Holes 173

Conclusion 191

Index ....

Preface

The robust restorative mechanism of the juvenile justice system in India, based on International set standards, consolidates therapeutic intervention through an informal judicial process for juvenile delinquents, and the creation of welfare agencies and children care homes. The principles embodied in the Juvenile Justice (Care and Protection Act, 2015 consider the child a national asset with the inability to comprehend the consequences of disproportionate conduct and recognises the detrimental impact of incarceration and corporal punishments. Various factors are responsible for the delinquent behavior of the juveniles.

Moreover, these factors are inter-linked to each other. Industrial development along with its positive effect for boosting the economy has also adversely affected the social life of the people. The foremost impact is the disintegration of joint family which resulted into lack of parental control. The purpose behind the discussion on the role of various factors of juvenile delinquency is to bring on notice that children lack the capacity to differentiate between right and wrong. This being the nature of juvenile delinquency, it was not considered proper to treat the young juvenile delinquent through regular criminal justice system applicable to all the adult criminals.

Thus, the particular need was felt to deal with them in such a way that could bring the reformation and rehabilitation along with the element of punishment. Accordingly, for their separate treatment, juvenile justice system in India came into existence which is considered as the integral part of the criminal justice system. This system is specially framed and established to extend special protections to children and young offender who have indulged into the criminal world. The protection extended to the children is in nature of positive protection towards reforming and rehabilitating their lives.

The objective behind observation homes which embodies principles of natural justice, repatriation, and non-stigmatization semantics is to provide differential treatment from adult offenders to prevent dwarfing the development of a child and coarsening of his conscience. However, the failure of the legal and administrative system makes juveniles stumble back and forth between the ever-evolving doors of reformative and retributive justice practices. The book analyses the discrepancies and lacunae in the administration of the rules stipulated, in India, and proposes potential domains of reformation.

1

Introduction

India is home to 472 million children in the age group of 0-18 years, constituting almost 39 per cent of the nation's population. Unfortunately, India is also home to many child labourers, homeless children, migrant children, run aways, orphans or abandoned children and victims of sexual and other forms of child abuse. According to the National Crime Records Bureau, there has been an over 13 per cent increase in crimes against children between 2015 and 2016 as against a 5.3 per cent increase between 2014 and 2015. Of course, there are many more that go unregistered and unrecorded.

Just as in other countries of the world, in India too, children commit offences. Crimes committed by children constituted 0.7 percent of all crimes in 2016, which was the same in 2015. IPC crimes committed by children has remained about 1 per cent of the total IPC crimes over the years. However, children who come in conflict with the law are a category that need attention and intervention so that they can be moved away from the world of crime and offence and placed back in society as responsible citizens.

The correlation between children who come in conflict

with the law, and those in need of care and protection, is a strongone. A large number of children (42 percent) apprehended, belonged to poor families whose annual income was up to only INR 25,000. Almost 46 per cent of the total children apprehended were either illiterate or had been only to primary school. Hence, addressing the needs of vulnerable children is critical to the prevention of crime by children.

Preventing crime by children and protecting them from becoming victims of crime, are both central to protecting children's rights. It is the recognition of this important fact that forms the bedrock of juvenile justice system in India, which has always addressed two categories of children – Children in Conflict with the Law (CICL) and Children in Need of Care and Protection (CNCP).

Since children live everywhere - in cities, towns and villages and as part of families and communities, the challenge in protecting them is to provide protective mechanisms and systems wherever they are. This calls for a well- defined, regulated and administered system of governance at different levels so that every last child can be reached. India is committed to safeguarding the rights of its children. The Constitution of India through various key provisions recognizes the vulnerabilities faced by children and upholds their right to protection. Article 15 (3) of the Constitution guarantees special attention to children through necessary and special laws and policies that safeguard their rights. The Right to equality, protection of life and personal liberty and the right against exploitation is enshrined in Articles 14 (right to equality), 15 (prohibition of discrimination), 17 (Abolition of untouchability), 21 (right to life and personal liberty), 23 (prohibition of trafficking) and 24 (prohibition of employment of children in factories etc).

The spirit of the State towards safeguarding its children is reflected in the key legislations for the protection of children i.e. Juvenile Justice (Care and Protection of Children) Act, 2015, Child Labour (Prohibition and Regulation) Act, 1986 (Amended in 2016), Right to Education Act, 2009 (Amended in 2012), and Prevention of Children from Sexual Offences Act, 2012 etc. Child rights and welfare concerns have also been addressed in a number of International Conventions and norms on child protection including the UN Convention on the Rights of the Child (UNCRC) 1989, the UN Standard Minimum Rules for the Administration of Juvenile Justice (The Beijing Rules), 1985, the UN Rules for the Protection of Juveniles Deprived of their Liberty, 1990, and the Hague Convention on Inter-country Adoption, 1993. The Government of India ratified the UN Convention on the Rights of the Child (UNCRC) in 1992.

The Juvenile Justice (Care and Protection of Children) Act, 2015 is the key legislation for juvenile justice in India. The Act emphasizes the rehabilitation and reintegration of children through various non-institutional and institutional measures. The Act recognizes the role of family care and support in the development of children and prescribes various measures for non-institutional care for children in difficult circumstances. It also provides a procedure for trial of children in conflict with law and the orders that can be passed by Juvenile Justice Board in case of children who are found guilty of commission of offence. Such children are either lodged in Observation Home, Special Home or Place of Safety under the said Act. The major change in the 2015 Act is the segregation of children who have perpetrated heinous crimes. The Act vests the JJB with discretion to decide whether a child between 16-18 years accused of committing a heinous crime is to be tried in the adult criminal justice system as opposed to the juvenile justice system.

The Hon'ble Supreme Court of India, in the matter of Re-inhuman conditions in 1382 prisons, observed and passed an order on 05.02.2016 to the following effect:

Taking a cue from the efforts of the Ministry of Home Affairs in preparing the Model Prison Manual, it appears advisable and necessary to ensure that a similar manual is prepared in respect of juveniles who are in custody either in Observation Homes or Special Homes or Places of Safety in terms of the Juvenile Justice (Care and Protection of Children) Act, 2015. The other important observations made in the judgment are with regard to upholding the fundamental rights of prisoners as human beings that respects their dignity and protects them from ill treatment and abuse. It is in this context that the Hon'ble Supreme Court of India directed the Ministry of Women and Child Development to prepare a Manual for the Care Givers of Child Care Institutions (CCIs) aimed at improving the standard of care and services to be provided in CCIs for children in conflict with law.

All children have specific needs and rights. It is a well-established fact that children have unique vulnerabilities owing to specific needs and demands at different stages of growth till the time they reach adulthood. Every child who comes in contact with the juvenile justice system is a child in difficult circumstances who has fallen out of the protective net at some point and has been robbed of an opportunity of a safe and secure childhood. Children in conflict with law should be treated as children in difficult circumstances and the approach of the juvenile justice system should be aimed at addressing the vulnerabilities of children and ensuring their rehabilitation. The Juvenile Justice (Care and Protection of Children) Act, 2015 promotes the institutionalization of children as a last resort. The institutionalization of children when necessary should be in the best interest of children, and aimed at educating, rehabilitating and preparing children for their re-integration into the society upon release. It is important that children, irrespective of the offences committed by them [or alleged to be committed by them], should be treated with respect and dignity while in custody in CCIs, focusing on their potential and capabilities as children. Studies indicate that the most effective way to find constructive solutions to involvement of children in activities that violate a law is to involve children in the process of rehabilitation and not to consider them as merely 'trouble makers' or 'problem children' in need of punishment. Recognition of and respect for their rights as human being and as a child is an important first step in this direction.

Even when in institutional care and deprived of liberty, the child is entitled to all rights as enshrined in UNCRC and the Juvenile Justice (Care and Protection of Children) Act, 2015. The standards of care and rehabilitation must be respected and upheld by the system as a whole including the connected government departments, the institution, and all care givers working with children in CCI. It is the responsibility of every care giver in a CCI to make maximum effort to ensure that the care given to children complements and complies with the provisions of the Juvenile Justice (Care and Protection of Children) Act, 2015 and the Rules made there under.

The Juvenile Justice (Care and Protection of Children) Act, 2015 and the Juvenile Justice (Care and Protection of Children) Model Rules, 2016 outline the standards of care for children in a CCI. The Manual outlines the standards of care and services in a structured manner and lays down processes to be followed from the time a child enters a CCI till he/she is transferred or released. The care givers in a CCI are expected to follow these standards of care while caring for children. The only distinction that the Juvenile Justice (Care and Protection of Children) Act, 2015 makes is for the three CCIs for children in conflict with law namely, observation home, special home and place of safety. The adherence to the standards of care and services apply to all care givers and organizations appointed and contracted by the Nodal Department implementing the J.J. Act at the State and District level, to provide care and rehabilitation to children in a CCI as per the Juvenile Justice (Care and Protection of Children) Act, 2015. Nothing in the Manual shall be in derogation to the JJ Act, 2015 and the JJ Model Rules, 2016.

The underlying thinking that underpins the guidance provided in this Manual, is that CCIs must strive to be vibrant centres which facilitate a process of transformation and healing in children. It includes recognition that every child is unique, with a unique set of needs and must be given as many options towards his/her rehabilitation; every interaction with a child must facilitate the process of taking responsibility, accountability for his/her actions and lead the child towards transformation; children must feel that they are respected, trusted, and listened to; CCIs must function as active members of communities with openness and transparency.

It is hoped that this Manual will help care givers understand how critical their roles are in helping young people address issues, take responsibility, pick themselves up and move forward with their lives in a healthy and productive manner. It is also hoped that this Manual will help government at all levels realize the significant role such institutions play in the reformation and rehabilitation of children in conflict with law. Further, this Manual will also contribute to the momentum towards strengthening capacities of CCIs and their human resources to deliver quality services to children in conflict with law.

This book contains information on the law, the history, principles which drive it; it provides an understanding on working with adolescents, children's participation in institutional settings, introduces restorative justice, the approach and philosophy of providing services to children in CCIs, details the roles and responsibilities of staff of CCIs, provides guidance on how to provide the range of services to children in CCIs, discusses monitoring, and outlines the roles which allied government departments can play in supporting CCIs to run effectively. The manual should be a work in progress updated over time with good practices and learning from CCIs across the country.

References

1. Jain, M. P. (2017). *Outlines of Indian Legal History*. NM Tripathi Private Ltd.
2. Ahuja, R. (2014). *Social Problems in India*. Rawat Publications.
3. UN General Assembly, *United Nations Standard Minimum Rules for the Treatment of Prisoners (the Nelson Mandela Rules)*
4. UN Commission on Human Rights, *Convention on the Rights of the Child.*
5. The Juvenile Justice (Care and Protection of Children) Act, 2015 (India)
6. India Jails Committee. (1921). *Report of the Indian Jails Committee, 1919-20.*
7. Court on Its Own Motion v. Dept. of Women and Child
8. Sheela Barse v. Union of India, (1986) 3 SCC 632
9. UN General Assembly, *International Covenant on Civil and Political Rights,* 16 December 1966, United Nations, Treaty Series, vol. 999.
10. Assembly, U. G. (1948). Universal Declaration of Human Rights. *UN General Assembly.*

2

Reason Behind Separate Treatment of Juveniles

Therapeutic jurisprudence is a perspective focusing on therapeutic or anti-therapeutic consequences of substantive laws, legal rules and procedures. The Juvenile Justice System is entrusted with the dual responsibility to follow specialized informal judicial process for juvenile delinquents, for remediation through therapeutic intervention, and to create community based welfare agencies for neglected juveniles. Such differential treatment for juvenile delinquents is not a phenomenon of recent origin and can be traced as far back as the code of Hammurabi in 2270 B.C. (Jain, 2017), and the Reformatory Schools Act, 1876. Delinquency includes any offence of robbery/theft, attempt to murder/murder, rape, addictions and any deviation from normal behavior such as truancy, vandalism, immorality and ungovernability (Ahuja, 1992).

Rise in juvenile delinquencies can be attributed to the wake of industrialization and urbanization due to unprecedented stress on social mobility and weakening of traditional means of social control. Such therapeutic intervention is based on the purpose to rejuvenate potential of juveniles to reintegrate them in the society through institutional and non-institutional measures.

Whether a person is actually involved in committing a crime, or is falsely accused of having done so - either way, such situations are generally ones that result in feelings of anxiety, fear and confusion. For a child/adolescent who is still growing and vulnerable, such a situation is naturally all the more challenging. Advocates working with children in conflict with law have a very noble and yet challenging task - one of building trust and faith in a young person who is in a very difficult circumstance, to who the advocate is a complete stranger, all the while ensuring that the legal duty to defend the client and protect all his/her rights and needs is diligently discharged. Approaches and skills adopted and decisions taken by advocates working with such children significantly influence the route these children will take and the experience they will have in their often arduous journey through the justice system. This Handbook provides examples of such an advocate can be instrumental in not only dramatically changing the course of a child's life, but also transforming and holding the juvenile justice system itself accountable to the children, whose best interest it is intended to serve. In this sense, the work that such advocates do in this field, and the results that accrue from it, also plays a vital role in influencing public perception about the juvenile justice system, as to whether or not it delivers the objectives of the laws that govern this area of practice.

A majority of children in conflict with law entering the Juvenile Justice System, hail from poor impoverished families. These children are entitled to justice, care, protection, treatment, development, rehabilitation and social re-integration, as envisaged in the Preamble of the Juvenile Justice (Care and Protection of Children) Act, 2015, (JJ Act,

2015). The Preamble, which lays out the object of the enactment, states that the law is to be implemented '....by adopting a child-friendly approach in the adjudication and disposal of matters in the best interest of children and for their rehabilitation...,' (emphasis added). The jurisprudence on juvenile justice in India that has informed the JJ Act, 2015 as well as the UN Convention on the Rights of the Child, 1989, acceded to by India in 1992, and the range of guidelines brought out by the United Nations on this topic; require advocates working with children in conflict with law to forge competencies that to a large extent, are a radical shift away from what constitutes regular practice in criminal matters. The sections below elucidate this point by capturing the essence of the legal framework governing this area of practice.

The right to legal aid for all persons alleged to be in conflict with law has been enshrined in the Constitution of India. Article 21 of the Constitution of India guarantees an accused the right to a fair trial; Article 22(1) guarantees anyone who is arrested, the right to consult and be defended by a legal practitioner of his choice; and Article 39-A requires the State to provide legal aid through suitable legislation or schemes to ensure that people are not deprived of the opportunity to secure justice due to economic or other disabilities. Under Sections 12(c) and 13, of The Legal Services Authorities Act, 1987, children and persons in custody are entitled to legal aid.

Article 40(1), of the UN Convention on the Rights of the Child, 1989, (UNCRC), which India acceded to in 1992, places an obligation to States Parties to recognize the right of every child alleged as, accused of, or recognized as having infringed the penal law to be treated in a manner consistent with the promotion of the child's sense of dignity and worth, which reinforces the child's respect for the human rights and fundamental freedoms of others.

Though the JJ Act, 2015 also deals with crimes committed by children it is a socially beneficial legislation, imposing duties on all those involved in administration of the law to align their work with the call arising out of its Preamble and the fundamental principles enshrined in Section 3. Advocates should also adhere to the fundamental principles enshrined under Section 3 of the JJ Act, 2015, -principles that all functionaries and authorities are required to abide by. In particular, advocates working with such children are required to adhere to the principle of best interests, i.e., Section 3(ix), which states – "All decisions regarding the child shall be based on the primary consideration that they are in the best interest of the child and to help the child to develop full potential". The advocate therefore has to ensure that this becomes the guiding force, one that should not be compromised or violated, irrespective of the gravity of the crime the child is alleged to have committed. The term "best interests" has been defined under Section 2(9), of the Act to mean – "the basis for any decision taken regarding the child, to ensure fulfilment of his basic rights and needs, identity, social well-being and physical, emotional and intellectual development,"(emphasis added).

The Juvenile Justice (Care and Protection) Act (2015) runs collateral to the United Nations Standard Minimum Rules for the administration of Juvenile Justice(1985) and Standard Minimum Rules for the Treatment of Prisoners (2016) adopted by the United Nations, ratified by India. The Beijing rules emphasize that the detention, arrest and imprisonment shall be the last resort for handling juveniles and if nevertheless used, they shall be detained in a separate (or part of) institution than adults, involving close supervision, intensive care and remediation. This resonates with the Standard Minimum Rules for the Treatment of

Prisoner which emphasize on the creation of semi-institutional arrangements such as half-way houses, educational homes, day-time training centre with a focus on rehabilitation and social re-integration of youth.

Robust mechanism of the Juvenile Justice (Care and Protection of Children) Act, 2015 acknowledges the aforesaid duty through the provisions which seek creation of Child Care Institutions to accord differential treatment for juvenile delinquents than the adult offenders. Section 2(21) of the Juvenile Justice(Care and Protection of Children) Act (2015) defines Child Care Institutions as,

> *"Children Home, Open Shelter, Observation Home, Special Home, Place of Safety, Specialised Adoption Agency and a Fit Facility recognized under the Act for providing care and protection to children, who are in need of such services."*

The essence of the Juvenile Justice [Care and Protection of Children] Act, 2015, and the Rules outlined in 2007, is restorative and not retributive, entails rehabilitation and reintegration of juveniles in conflict with law, into standard society (Sahil Bilal v Union of India, 2013). Therefore, in pursuance of the aforesaid rules, Observation Homes, according the JJ Act are meant for temporary reception, care and rehabilitation of any juvenile alleged to be in conflict with the law, during the pendency of any inquiry against him/her. Observation home means an observation home established and maintained in every district or group of districts by a state government, either by itself, or through a voluntary or non-governmental organization, and is registered as such, for the purposes specified in the Act (The Juvenile (Care and Protection) Act, 2015).

Thus, observation homes play the major role of rehabilitating the delinquent juveniles by providing environmental attributes which rejuvenate the potential of the juveniles to re-integrate into the society. The functioning of observation homes embodies principles of therapeutic jurisprudence, reformative justice to mitigate potential downstream detrimental impact of incarceration and corporal punishments.

References

1. Delhi High Court Juvenile Justice Committee. (2006). *Brief note on constitution and functioning of juvenile justice committee.*

2. The Juvenile Justice (Care and Protection of Children) Model Rules, 2016

3. Parackal, S., & Panicker, R. (2019). *Children and Crime in India: Causes, Narratives and Interventions.*

4. UN Committee on the Rights of the Child (CRC), *General comment No. 12 (2009): The right of the child to be heard.*

5. Kapil, U. (2002). Integrated Child Development Services (ICDS) Scheme: a program for holistic development of children in India. *The Indian Journal of Pediatrics, 69*(7), 597-601.

6. Department for Women, Children, Disabled and Senior Citizens. (2016). *Audit Report on 'General & Social Sector' for the year 2015, Chapter III Compliance Audit Observations.*

7. Agarwal, D. (2018). Juvenile Delinquency in India-Latest Trends and Entailing Amendments in Juvenile Justice Act People: International Journal of Social Sciences, 3(3)1365-1383.

8. Agarwal, D. D. (2017). Juvenile delinquency in India – Latest Trends and Entailing Amendments in Juvenile Justice act. University School of Law and Legal Studies, Delhi, India Vol 3.

3

Doli Incapax and Age of Child: A Dilemma

In India, the Census of India defines persons below the age of fourteen as children. When making use of standard demographic data, social scientists include females in the age group of fifteen to nineteen years under the category of the girl child. Most of the government programmes on children are targeted for the age group below fourteen years. According to the Constitution, 'no child below the age of fourteen years shall be employed to work in any factory or mine or engaged in any other hazardous employment'. The legal conception of a child has tended to vary depending upon the purpose. A few illustrations from the law in India are given below:

1. **Criminal Law**: Indian Penal Code, 1860: Nothing is an offence, which is done by a child under the age of 7 years. The age of criminal responsibility is raised to 12 years if the child is found to have not attained the ability to understand the nature and consequences of his/ her act. Attainment of sixteen years of age for a girl is necessary for giving sexual consent, which is not less than fifteen years in case she is married.

2. **Juvenile Law**: Juvenile Justice Act, 1960: A juvenile is a child who has not completed the age of 18 years. A delinquent juvenile cannot be sentenced to imprisonment. If a juvenile who has attained the age of 16 years commits an offence of a serious nature and is found not to be in his interest or in the interest of other juveniles to send him to a special home then the juvenile court may order the delinquent juvenile to be kept in safe custody in such place and manner as it thinks fit. Detention in police stations or jails is specifically prohibited under the Act.

The word "child" has been used in various legislations as a term denoting relationship; as a term indicating capacity; and as a term of special protection. These alternative specifications give different concepts about the Child. These include viewing children as a burden which invokes rights to maintenance and support; regarding children as undergoing temporary disabilities making for rights to special treatment and special discrimination; treating children as specially vulnerable for ensuring rights of protection; and recognizing children as resources for the country's development necessitating their nurturing and advancement.

Legal enactments invoke differential age-specifics, creating a dilemma whether the same human being is or is not a child and, depends upon the law which is being invoked in a given case. Given the fact that the deprived child's birth is either inadequately/ incorrectly recorded, the reliability and impact of the laws thus cannot be fully regulated in terms of age. The laws which relate to transgression by the child, are under the general rubric of.

Juvenile, while distinguishes treatment vis-a-vis the adult, for offences like begging/ stealing/ drug taking/ peddling or crime. Free legal aid is available, under the Public Utility Litigation provisions. But the disparity between the age identified child and the laws applicable in terms of maturity levels and the child's ability to articulate needs requires congruent thinking in policy, laws statements and their enactments.

The Doctrine of Doli Incapax

Doli Incapax is a doctrine that propounds the incapability of a wrong doer on various basis, juvenility being one of them. Since a long time, the legislators and eventually court have been interpreting juvenility on the basis of age only but now there is an evident paradigm shift wherein the court are trying to establish juvenility not only biologically but also mentally. India being a welfare state, is under a continuous obligation to uphold the wellbeing of juveniles yet the range of crimes, the gravity and atrocity of the crimes committed by the juveniles propel us all to think the etiology of the crimes committed by the juveniles and how much justified would it be to give them the benefit of doli incapax. The legal system related to juvenile justice is transforming and the court are willing to rebut the contentions of doli incapax of juveniles based on the age only.

Doli incapax is a Latin term that means "incapable of doing harm" and the concept is used in order to establish the presumption about the innocence for children in Criminal law. The basis of this presumption is the theory of Criminal responsibility that a person should be held criminally responsible only for acts he intends to commit. In India the Code of Criminal Procedure recognises, Doli incapax and provides that there is a line (age line) below which children are not truly capable of criminal behaviour because they are incapable of the requisite moral and cognitive process which is called as "qualified immunity". Culpability is a pre-requisite for the criminal laws to be imposed and culpability is generally assumed to be present except in the cases of excuses as insanity or duress. Every person who has the ability to reason and distinguish between right or wrong has to bear the responsibility of all the actions done by him. If a wrong is being committed causing damage to other person a man has to bear the responsibility on the basis of culpability. The damage caused by a minor can be just as real as that of a grownup but before coming to a conclusion or trying a minor same as that of an adult a general test needs to be performed to ascertain the child has adequate understanding of the likely consequence of the act. Any contributory negligence by a child is to be judged by the standards of a child and not as per the criterion of reasonable adult.

The entire juvenile justice mechanism entails the establishment of one factor i.e. juvenility which eventually proves Doli incapax of a person. Juvenility predominantly is associated withthe natal age of a human being which again is uncluttered and inferred in various ways to which recently judiciary has integrated other facets of a person that need to be considered in order to substantiate juvenility. In the words of Lord Scarman, Gillick, "The law must be sensitive to human development and social change."

Legal basis for fixing the age in the Juvenile Justice Act, 2015 or IPC or Cr.P.C is in tune with the provisions of the Constitution. The basis of fixing of the age is more biological than based on culpabilities or intentions. There are many variables in the context of juvenility generated Doli incapax.

India is still struggling with digitalisation and data compilation of the Indian Residents making it quite hard to even find the evidences or documents proving the biological age, accessible.The courts have time and again tried to find ways to establish the prima facie requirement i.e. biological age in order to establish juvenility.

The Supreme Court in the matter of Shah Nawaz v. State of Uttar Pradesh & Anr., (2011) 13 SCC 751, while examining the meaning and mode of determination of age of a delinquent 'Juvenile' under the Juvenile Justice (Care and Protection of Children) Rules, 2007 said inter alia, "Before considering the merits of the claim of the appellant and the stand of the State, let us consider Rule 12 of the Juvenile Justice (Care and Protection of Children) Rules, 2007 (hereinafter referred to as 'the Rules') which reads as under:

> "12. Procedure to be followed in determination of Age.
>
> (1) In every case concerning a child or a juvenile in conflict with law, the court or the Board or as the case may be the Committee referred to in rule 19 of these rules shall determine the age of such juvenile or child or a juvenile in conflict with law within a period of thirty days from the date of making of the application for that purpose.
>
> (2) The court or the Board or as the case may be the Committee shall decide the juvenility or otherwise of the juvenile or the child or as the case may be the juvenile in conflict with law, prima facie on the basis of physical appearance or documents, if available, and send him to the observation home or in jail.
>
> (3) In every case concerning a child or juvenile in conflict with law, the age determination inquiry shall be conducted by the court or the Board or, as the case may be, the Committee by seeking evidence by obtaining –
>
> (a) (i) the matriculation or equivalent certificates, if available; and in the absence whereof;
>
> (ii) the date of birth certificate from the school (other than a play school) first attended; and in the absence whereof;
>
> (iii) the birth certificate given by a corporation or a municipal authority or a panchayat;

(b) and only in the absence of either (i), (ii) or (iii) of clause (a) above, the medical opinion will be sought from a duly constituted Medical Board, which will declare the age of the juvenile or child. In case exact assessment of the age cannot be done, the Court or the Board or, as the case may be, the Committee, for the reasons to be recorded by them, may, if considered necessary, give benefit to the child or juvenile by considering his/her age on lower side within the margin of one year. and, while passing orders in such case shall, after taking into consideration such evidence as may be available, or the medical opinion, as the case may be, record a finding in respect of his age and either of the evidence specified in any of the clauses (a)(i), (ii), (iii) or in the absence whereof, clause (b) shall be the conclusive proof of the age as regards such child or the juvenile in conflict with law.

(4) If the age of a juvenile or child or the juvenile in conflict with law is found to be below 18 years on the date of offence, on the basis of any of the conclusive proof specified in sub-rule (3), the court or the Board or as the case may be the Committee shall in writing pass an order stating the age and declaring the status of juvenility or otherwise, for the purpose of the Act and these rules and a copy of the order shall be given to such juvenile or the person concerned.

(5) Save and except where, further inquiry or otherwise is required, inter alia, in terms of section 7A, section 64 of the Act and these rules, no further inquiry shall be conducted by the court or the Board after examining and obtaining the certificate or any other documentary proof referred to in sub-rule (3) of this rule.

(6) The provisions contained in this rule shall also apply to those disposed off cases, where the status of juvenility has not been determined in accordance with the provisions contained in sub-rule (3) and the Act,

> requiring dispensation of the sentence under the Act for passing appropriate order in the interest of the juvenile in conflict with law."

Raju and Anr. v. State of Haryana, (2010) 3 SCC 235 was the case where the Court had admitted "mark sheet" as one of the proof in determining the age of the accused person while in Hari Ram v. State of Rajasthan & Anr.(2009) 13 SCC 211, court held that the juvenile claiming Doli incapax must be a minor on the date of the incident and only then the provisions of the Juvenile Justice Act would apply in his case.In Bhoop Ram v. State of U.P.(1989) 3 SCC 1 and in many other cases like; Rajinder Chandra vs. State of Chhattisgarh and Anr. (2002) 2 SCC 287, Ravinder Singh Gorkhi vs. State of U.P. (2006) 5 SCC, Pradeep Kumar vs. State of U.P. 1995 Supp (4) SCC 419, the Court while considering whether the appellant was entitled to the lesser imprisonment and should be treated as a "child" within the meaning of Section 2(4) of the U.P. Children Act, 1951 (1 of 1952 relied on the entry made in the column "date of birth" in the School Leaving Certificate.

In Arnit Das v. State of Bihar, (2000) 5 SCC 488, this Court admitted that the question of determination of the age of an accused, for the purpose of finding out whether he is a juvenile or not, technical and intricate and hence if two views may be possible on the same evidence, the court should lean in favour of holding the accused to be juvenile giving him due benefit of doubt and to uphold his welfare.

The Supreme Court in Abuzar Hossain @ Gulam Hossain v. State of West Bengal, (2012) 10 SCC 489. summarised the legal position as, "Delinquent juveniles need to be dealt with differently from adults. International covenants and domestic laws in various countries have prescribed minimum standards for delinquent juveniles and juveniles in conflict with law. These standards provide what orders may be passed regarding delinquent juveniles and the orders that may not be passed against them. This group of matters raises the question of when a claim of juvenility should, be recognised and sent for determination when it is raised for the first time in appeal or before this Court or raised in trial and appeal but not pressed and then pressed for the first time before this Court or even raised for the first time after final disposal of the case."

Doli Incapax: Rebuttable Presumption and Adult Responsibility in Juveniles

Professor Colin Howard in his book entitled Criminal Law, 4th ed. (1982), P. 343, Quoted by Harper J; R (A Child) v Whitty, (1993) A Crim R 462. said, "No civilised society regards children as accountable for their actions to the same extent as adults' The wisdom of protecting young children against the full rigour of the law is beyond argument. The difficulty lies in determining when and under what circumstances should it be removed."

The presumption of Doli Incapax may be an element of the prosecution case but is not a defence.The prosecution must rebut the presumption of Doli incapax as an element of the prosecution case specifically when reasonably the child knew the act was seriously wrong as opposed to naughty. Recently the Indian justice system have witnessed the change in the conceptualisation of Doli incapax in the cases of juveniles specifically.

Courts recently have shown courage to rebut the presumption of Doli incapax only on the basis of age and have started analysing the mental capabilities of the juveniles in question. One such landmark discussion was witnessed in the matter of Subramanian Swamy and others v. Raju through member, Juvenile Justice Board and another, (2013) 10 SCC 465, AIR 2014 (SC) 1649, where the hon'ble Supreme

Court although observed that elaborate statistics had been laid before them showing the extent of serious crimes committed by juveniles and the increase in the rate of such crimes, of late but still refused to be tempted to enter into the said arena which is primarily for the legislature to consider. The juvenility based Doli incapax was argued in a very comprehensive manner by Dr. Subramanian Swamy including not only biological but mental elements in the consideration. He clarified that he was neither challenging the provisions of Section 2(k) and 2(l) of the Juvenile Justice Act, 2000 nor was he invoking the jurisdiction of the Court to strike down any other provision of the Act or for interference of the Court to reduce the minimum age of juveniles fixed under the Act as 18 years. He wanted to highlight the object behind the enactment and contended that the Act was to be read down to understand that the true test of "juvenility" is not in the age but in the level of mental maturity of the offender. He strongly believed through his contentions that an object could save the Act from unconstitutionality.

He further emphasized that the act was not intended to apply to serious or heinous crimes committed by a juvenile. The provisions of Sections 82 and 83 of the Indian Penal Code were also argued on the basis that while a child below 7 cannot be held to be criminally liable, the criminality of those between 7 and 12 years is to be judged by the level of their mental maturity. He asserted that the same principle can be applied to all children beyond 12 and upto 18 years making IPC and JJ Act harmonious to each other. Further, Dr. Swamy contended that the Act will offend Article 14 of the Constitution if all the offenders below the age of 18 years irrespective of the degree/level of mental maturity and irrespective of the gravity of the crime committed would be treated at par. Such a blanket treatment of all offenders below the age of 18 committing any offence, regardless of the seriousness and depravity, is wholly impermissible under our constitutional scheme. Dr. Swamy urged that the relevant provisions of the Act i.e. Sections 1(4), 2(k), 2(l) and Section 7 must be read in such a way that juveniles (children below the age of 18) who are intellectually, emotionally and mentally mature enough to understand the implications of their acts and who have committed serious crimes do not come under the purview of the Act. He said, "Such juveniles are liable to be dealt with under the penal law of the country and by the regular hierarchy of courts under the criminal justice system administered in India. This is what was intended by the legislature; a plain reading, though, shows an unintended omission which must be made up or furnished by the Court".

It is further urged that not reading the Act in such manner out would render the same in breach of Article 14 as inasmuch as in that event there would be a blanket/flat categorisation of all juveniles, regardless of their mental and intellectual maturity, committing any offence, regardless of its seriousness, in one homogenous block in spite of their striking dissimilarities. As per Dr. Swamy contentions, a classification beyond what would be permissible under Article 14 if such classification does not further the targeted object i.e. to confer the benefits of the Act to persons below 18 who are not criminally responsible in view of the low level of mental maturity reached or achieved.

Another breakthrough happened after the unfortunate Nirbhaya case (as it was known). It was after this case that juvenility on the basis of age only was questioned widely and a Verma Committee was constituted to propose amendments not only regarding trials and punishments in case of juveniles in conflict of law but criminal justice system largely. The Committee gave in its findings and on the Reduction of age in respect of juveniles the committee proposed in Report of the Committee on Amendments to

Criminal Law, Submitted by Justice J.S. Verma (Retired), the Chairman of the Committee on January 23, 2013.

> "We have heard experts on the question of reduction of the age of a juvenile from 18 to 16 for the purpose of being tried for offences under various laws of the country. We must confess that the degree of maturity displayed by all the women's organizations, the academics and a large body of thinking people have viewed this incident both in the criminological as well as societal perspective humbles us."

Assuming that a person at the age of 16 is sent to life imprisonment, he would be released sometimes in the mid-30s. There is little assurance that the convict would emerge a reformed person, who will not commit the same crime that he was imprisoned for (or, for that matter, any other crime). The attempt made by Ms. Kiran Bedi to reform Tihar Jail inmates was, and continues to be, that is only a flash in the pan. Our jails do not have reformatory and rehabilitation policies. We do not engage with inmates as human beings. We do not bring about transformation. We, therefore, breed more criminals including juveniles) in our prison and reformatory system by forcing them in juvenile homes and protective homes where they are told that the State will protect and provide for them, but which promise is a fruitless one.

Children, who have been deprived of parental guidance and education, have very little chances of mainstreaming and rehabilitations, with the provisions of the Juvenile Justice Act being reduced to words on paper. We are of the view that the 3 year period (for which delinquent children are kept in the custody of special home) is cause for correction with respect to the damage done to the personality of the child. We are completely dissatisfied with the operation of children's institutions and it is only the magistrate (as presiding officer of the Juvenile Justice Board) who seems to be taking an interest in the situation. The sheer lack of counselors and therapy has divided the younger society into 'I' and 'them'.

We have also taken note of the fact that considering the recidivism being 8.2% in the year 2010, as against 6.9% during 2011, we are not inclined to reduce the age of a juvenile to 16.

It is time that the State invested in reformation for juvenile offenders and destitute juveniles. There are numerous jurisdictions like the United Kingdom, Thailand, and South Africa where children are corrected and rehabilitated; restorative justice is done and abuse is prevented. We think this is possible in India but it requires a determination of a higher order."

The committee analysed Articles 37 and 38 of the Convention on the Rights of Child and certain scientific factors were also taken into account. Committee having regard to the development in neurosciences, expressed its view, that adolescent brain development is one of the important issues in public policy as per the Verma Committee Report. The reference was given by the committee, of the reasons stated by the US Supreme Court for abolishing death penalty for juveniles in Roper v. Simmons, 543 U.S. 551 (2005),wherein it was quoted as follows:

> "When a juvenile offender commits a heinous crime, the State can exact forfeiture of some of the most basic liberties, but the State cannot extinguish his life and his potential to attain a mature understanding of his own humanity. Retribution is not proportional if the law's most severe penalty is imposed on one whose culpability or blameworthiness is diminished, to a substantial degree, by reason of youth and immaturity."

After the "Nirbhaya" case, the Juvenile Justice (Care and Protection of Children) Act, 2015 was also amended in

2016 and a child in conflict with law over the age of 16 years, if charged with a heinous offence, can be tried in a court of law if the Juvenile Justice Board feels that he was mature enough to commit a crime.

India being a welfare state many times faces dilemma as to what extent a law should be a welfare and protective law and when should the law take stringent decisions to sanction and uphold the command. As much as a naïve juvenile needs protection and rehabilitation a shrewd juvenile need to be punished. This makes the task of establishment of Doli incapax element in case of juveniles difficult and rebuttal of the element even more technical and difficult.

In the words of Harper J., mentioned in Doli incapax - The Criminal Responsibility of Children, A paper by Matthew Johnston, barrister Forbes Chambers, Sydney for the Children's Magistrates' "The wisdom of protecting children from the full rigour of the law is beyond argument. The difficulty lies in determining when and under what circumstances protection should be removed."

References

1. AWG Kean, 'History of the Criminal Liability of Children' (1937) 53 Law Quarterly Review 364;

2. P Blazey-Ayoub, 'Doli Incapax' (1996) 30 Criminal Law Journal 34; T Crofts, 'Rebutting the Presumption of Doli Incapax' (1998) 62 Journal of Criminal Law 185;

3. T Bartholomew, 'Legal and Clinical Enactment of the Doli Incapax Defence in the Supreme Court of Victoria, Australia' (1998) 5(1) Psychiatry, Psychology and Law 95.

4. See eg Law Reform Commission of Hong Kong, *The Age of Criminal Responsibility in Hong Kong*, Consultation Paper, 1999

5. T Crofts, 'Doli Incapax: Why Children Deserve its Protection' [2003] Murdoch University Electronic Journal of Law 26.

4

Reason Behind Juvenile Delinquency

The problem of juvenile delinquency is gradually rearing up in its ugly head in the wake of industrialisation and urbanization in the country. As a result of various scientific and technological advances during the present century, the structure and functions of our society have undergone a change with the concomitant disorganisation and maladjustment. The growth of cities and heterogeneous population, great mobility and fluidity, occupational and cultural variations and over crowed conditions has given rise to new ways of living. Juveniles are affected in an unusual way by these changing conditions.

With rapid changes in socio-economic lives, unprecedented stress on materialistic culture, rapid increase in social mobility and weakening of the traditional means of social control, are to some extent responsible for the growth of juvenile delinquency in India. In most of the cases social deviance among children found to have been preceded by various phases of abandonment, destitution, neglect, truancy. vagrancy, abuse or exploitation.

This aspect, however does not establish the fact that poverty per se is a cause of problem. Children of the poor do not necessarily commit crime nor are those of the rich always law-abiding deprive a bulk of child. But the fact remains that poverty does deprive a bulk of from an equitable sharing of socio-cultural and economic opportunities which are necessary for their growth and development. These children are rendered vulnerable to social maladjustment and their eventual induction into criminogenic culture. It therefore becomes imperative that an effective system to prevent and control juvenile delinquency ought to be devised so that the problems with which they are confronted, are sorted out.

There is one major psychological theory – Social Learning Theory, which seeks to explain the causes of a particular behaviour. Followers of this theory see crime as a deliberate response to a particular life event. The most famous representative of this theory A. Bandura believed that people are not born with innate actions, and that violence and aggression can be learned by modelling the behaviour of others. Most times, the causes of the crime indeed can be linked to this theory. Especially in the cases of minors.

Unplanned Urbanization

Industrial development and economic growth has resulted in urbanization. This in turn resulted in the migration of large population from village to urban area. It resulted in new problems such as housing, slum dwelling, overcrowding, etc. The high cost of living in urban areas makes it necessary even for women to take outdoor jobs for supporting their families financially. This results in the neglect of children and ineffective or almost nil parental control. The temptation of luxuries of life lures young people and they may act in the wrong way to satisfy their wants. Thus unplanned urbanization is one of the important causes of juvenile delinquency:

A large number of individual factors and characteristics has been associated with the development of juvenile delinquency. These individual factors include age, gender, complications during pregnancy and delivery, impulsivity, aggressiveness, and substance use. Some factors operate before birth (prenatal) or close to, during, and shortly after birth (perinatal); some can be identified in early childhood; and other factors may not be evident until late childhood or during adolescence. To fully appreciate the development of these individual characteristics and their relations to delinquency, one needs to study the development of the individual in interaction with the environment. In order to simplify presentation of the research, however, this section deals only with individual factors.

Age

Studies of criminal activity by age consistently find that rates of offending begin to rise in preadolescence or early adolescence, reach a peak inlate adolescence, and fall through young adulthood. Some lawbreaking experience at some time during adolescence is nearly universal in American children, although much of this behaviour is reasonably mild and temporary. Although the exact age of onset, peak, and age of desistance varies by offense, the general pattern has been remarkably consistent over time, in different countries, and for official and self-reported data. For example, In a longitudinal study of a sample of boys in London (the Cambridge Longitudinal Study), found an eightfold increase in the number of different boys convicted of delinquent behavior from age 10 to age 17, followed by a decrease to a quarter of the maximum level by age 24. The number of self-reported offenses in the same sample also peaked between ages 15 and 18, then dropped sharply by age 24. In a longitudinal study of, the percentage of boys who self-reported serious delinquent behaviour rose from 5 percent at age 6 to about 18 percent for whites and 27 percent for blacks at age 16. A longitudinal study of a representative sample from high-risk neighbourhoods in Denver also found a growth in the self-reported prevalence of serious violence from age through late adolescence. Females in the Denver sample exhibited a peak in serious violence in mid-adolescence, but prevalence continued to increase through age 19 for the boys. The study is continuing to follow these boys to see if their prevalence drops in early adulthood. Using the Gluecks' data on 500 juvenile offenders from the 1940s, it was found that only 25 percent of them were still offending by age 32.

Prenatal and Perinatal Factors

Several studies have found an association between prenatal and perinatal complications and later delinquent or criminal behavior Prenatal and perinatal risk factors represent a host of latent and manifest conditions that influence subsequent development.

Many studies use the terms "prenatal or perinatal complications" to describe what is a very heterogeneous set of latent and clinical conditions. Under the heading of prenatal factors, one finds a broad variety of conditions that occurs before birth through the seventh month of gestation. Similarly, perinatal factors include conditions as varied as apnea of prematurity (poor breathing) to severe respiratory distress syndrome. The former condition is relatively benign, while the latter is often life-threatening. Although they are risk factors, low birthweight and premature birth do not necessarily presage problems in development.

Prenatal and perinatal risk factors may compromise the nervous system, creating vulnerabilities in the child that can lead to abnormal behavior. Children with prenatal and perinatal complications who live in impoverished, deviant, or abusive environments face added difficulties. According to three major large-scale, long-term studies:

(1) developmental risks have additive negative effects on child outcomes,

(2) most infants with perinatal complications develop into normally functioning children, and

(3) children with long-term negative outcomes who suffered perinatal complications more often than not came from socially disadvantaged backgrounds

Most measures indicate that males are more likely to commit crimes. They are also more vulnerable to prenatal and perinatal stress, as is shown through studies of negative outcomes, including death. Hyperactivity, attention problems, and impulsiveness in children have been found to be associated with delinquency. These behaviors can be assessed very early in life and are associated with certain prenatal and perinatal histories. For example, exposure to environmental toxins, such as prenatal lead exposure at very low levels, tends to adversely affect neonatal motor and attentional performance. Hyperactivity and aggression are associated with prenatal alcohol exposure. Prenatal exposure to alcohol, cocaine, heroin, and nicotine appear to have similar effects. Each tends to be associated with hyperactivity, attention deficit, and impulsiveness.

Individual Capabilities, Competencies, and Characteristics

In recent investigations, observable behaviors, such as duration of attention to a toy and compliance with mother's instructions not to touch an object, that are particularly relevant to later misbehavior are observable in the first year of life. However, the ability to predict behavior at later ages (in adolescence and adulthood) from such traits early in life is not yet known. Aggressive behavior is nevertheless one of the more stable dimensions, and significant stability may be seen from toddlerhood to adulthood.

The social behaviors that developmentalists study during childhood can be divided into two broad categories: prosocial and antisocial. Prosocial behaviors include helping, sharing, and cooperation, while antisocial behaviors include different forms of oppositional and aggressive behavior. The development of empathy, guilt feelings, social cognition, and moral reasoning are generally considered important emotional and cognitive correlates of social development.

Impulsivity and hyperactivity have both been associated with later antisocial behavior. The social behavior characteristics that best predict delinquent behavior, however, are physical aggression and oppositionality. Most children start manifesting these behaviors between the end of the first and second years. The peak level in frequency of physical aggression is generally reached between 24 and 36 months, an age at which the consequences of the aggression are generally relatively minor. By entry into kindergarten, the majority of children have learned to use other means than physical aggression to get what they want and to solve conflicts. Those who have not learned, who are oppositional and show few prosaical behaviors toward peers, are at high risk of being rejected by their peers, of failing in school, and eventually of getting involved in serious delinquency.

The differentiation of emotions and emotional regulation occurs during the 2-year period, from 12 months to 36 months, when the frequency of physical aggression increases sharply and then decreases almost as sharply. A number of longitudinal studies have shown that children who are behaviourally inhibited (shy, anxious) are less at risk of juvenile delinquency, while children who tend to be fearless, those who are impulsive, and those who have difficulty delaying gratification are more at risk of delinquent behaviour.

A large number of studies report that delinquents have a lower verbal IQ compared with non-delinquents, as well as lower school achievement. Antisocial youth also tend to show cognitive deficits in the areas of executive functions, perception of social cues, and problem-solving processing patterns. The association between cognitive deficits and delinquency remains after controlling for social class and race. Few studies, however, have assessed cognitive functioning during the preschool years or followed the children into adolescence to understand the long-term link between early cognitive deficits and juvenile delinquency. The studies that did look at children's early cognitive development have shown that poor language performance by the second year after birth, poor fine motor skills by the third year, and low IQ by kindergarten were all associated with later antisocial behavior. Stattin and Klackenberg-Larsson (1993) found that the association between poor early language performance and later criminal behavior remained significant even after controlling for socio-economic status.

Family Influences

In assigning responsibility for childrearing to parents, most Western cultures place a heavy charge on families. Such cultures assign parents the task of raising children to follow society's rules for acceptable behavior. It should be no surprise, therefore, when families have difficulties with the task laid on them, that the product often is juvenile delinquency. Family structure (who lives in a household) and family functioning (how the family members treat one another) are two general categories under which family effects on delinquency have been examined.

Family Structure

Before embarking on a review of the effects of family

structure, it is important to raise the question of mechanisms. It may not be the family structure itself that increases the risk of delinquency, but rather some other factor that explains why that structure is present. Alternatively, a certain family structure may increase the risk of delinquency, but only as one more stressor in a series; it may be the number rather than specific nature of the stressors that is harmful.

Historically, one aspect of family structure that has received a great deal of attention as a risk factor for delinquency is growing up in a family that has experienced separation or divorce. Although many studies have found an association between broken homes and delinquency, there is considerable debate about the meaning of the association. For example, longitudinal studies have found an increased level of conduct disorder and behavioral disturbance in children of divorcing parents before the divorce took place. Capaldi and Patterson (1991) showed that disruptive parenting practices and antisocial personality of the parent(s) accounted for apparent effects of divorce and remarriage. Thus, it is likely that the increased risk of delinquency experienced among children of broken homes is related to the family conflict prior to the divorce or separation, rather than to family breakup itself. In their longitudinal study of family disruption, Juby and Farrington (2001) found that boys who stayed with their mothers following disruption had delinquency rates that were almost identical to those reared in intact families.

Being born and raised in a single-parent family has also been associated with increased risk of delinquency and antisocial behavior. Research that takes into account the socio-economic conditions of single-parent households and other risks, including disciplinary styles and problems in supervising and monitoring children, show that these other factors account for the differential outcomes in these families. The important role of socio-economic conditions is shown by the absence of differences in delinquency between children in single-parent and two-parent homes within homogeneous socioeconomic classes. Careful analyses of juvenile court cases in the United States shows that economic conditions rather than family composition influenced children 's delinquency.

Statistical controls for the mothers' age and poverty have been found to remove effects attributed to single-parent families. Furthermore, the significance of being born to a single mother has changed dramatically over the past 30 years. In 1970, 10.7 percent of all births in the United States were to unmarried women. By 1997, births to unmarried women accounted for 32.4 percent of U.S. births. As Rutter and colleagues noted about similar statistics in the United Kingdom: "It cannot be assumed that the risks for antisocial behavior (from being born to a single parent) evident in studies of children born several decades ago will apply to the present generation of births." Recent work seems to bear out this conclusion. Gorman-Smith and colleagues found no association between single parenthood and delinquency in a poor, urban U.S. community.

Family Interaction

Even in intact, two-parent families, children may not receive the supervision, training, and advocacy needed to ensure a positive developmental course. A number of studies have found that poor parental management and disciplinary practices are associated with the development of delinquent behavior. Failure to set clear expectations for children's behavior, inconsistent discipline, excessively severe or aggressive discipline, and poor monitoring and supervision of children predict later delinquency. As Patterson indicates through his research, parents who nag or use idle threats are likely to generate coercive systems in which children gain control through misbehaving. Several longitudinal studies investigating the effects of punishment on aggressive behavior have shown that physical punishments are more likely to result in defiance than compliance. Perhaps the best grounds for believing that family interaction influences delinquency are programs that alter parental management techniques and thereby benefit siblings as well as reduce delinquent behavior by the child whose conduct brought the parents into the program.

Social Setting

Where a family lives affects the nature of opportunities that will be available to its members. In some communities, public transportation permits easy travel for those who do not own automobiles. Opportunities for employment and entertainment extend beyond the local boundaries. In other communities, street-corner gatherings open possibilities for illegal activities. Lack of socially acceptable opportunities leads to frustration and a search for alternative means to success. Community-based statistics show high correlations among joblessness, household disruption, housing density, infant deaths, poverty, and crime.

Community variations may account for the fact that some varieties of family life have different effects on delinquency in different communities. In general, consistent friendly parental guidance seems to protect children from delinquency regardless of neighborhoods. But poor socialization practices seem to be more potent in disrupted neighborhoods.

Neighborhoods influence children's behavior by providing examples of the values that people hold, and these examples influence children's perception of what is acceptable behavior. Communities in which criminal activities are common tend to establish criminal behavior as acceptable. Tolerance for gang activities varies by community.

In sum, family life influences delinquency in a variety

of ways. Children reared by affectionate, consistent parents are unlikely to commit serious crimes either as juveniles or as adults. Children reared by parents who neglect or reject them are likely to be greatly influenced by their community environments. When communities offer opportunities for and examples of criminal behavior, children reared by neglecting or rejecting parents are more likely to become delinquents. And delinquents are likely to become inadequate parents.

Peer Influences

A very robust finding in the delinquency literature is that antisocial behavior is strongly related to involvement with deviant peers. One longitudinal study reported that involvement with antisocial peers was the only variable that had a direct effect on subsequent delinquency other than prior delinquency. Factors such as peer delinquent behavior, peer approval of deviant behavior, attachment or allegiance to peers, time spent with peers, and peer pressure for deviance have all been associated with adolescent antisocial behavior. In other words, the effects of deviant peers on delinquency are heightened if adolescents believe that their peers approve of delinquency, if they are attached to those peers, if they spend much time with them, and if they perceive pressure from those peers to engage in delinquent acts.

There is a dramatic increase during adolescence in the amount of time adolescents spend with their friends, and peers become increasingly important during this developmental period. Moreover, peers appear to be most important during late adolescence, with their importance peaking at about age 17 and declining thereafter. Thus the decline in delinquency after about age 18 parallels the decline in the importance of peers, including those with deviant influences. Consistent with this view, in the longitudinal research of antisocial British youth by West and Farrington, deviant youth reported that withdrawal from delinquent peer affiliations was an important factor in desistance from offending. Peer influences appear to have a particularly strong relationship to delinquency in the context of family conflict.

References

1. Dr. Sunil K. Bhattacharya, Juvenile delinquency-An Indian Scenario.

2. Pradheepa P and K Murlidharan, Juvenile Delinquency – a socio-economic and family perspective. Social Welfare. 2005

3. Asian Development Bank (2018). Poverty in India.

4. Blokland, A.A. and Palmen, H. (2012). Criminal career patterns. In R. Loeber, M. Hoeve, N.W. Slot and Peter.

5. H. Van Der Laan (Eds.), Persisters and Desisters in Crime from adolescence into adulthood: Explanation,prevention and punishment, (pp. 13-50).

6. USA: Routledge.Chesney-Lind, M. (1988). Girls and status offenses: Is Juvenile Justice still sexist? Criminal Justice Abstracts.

5

Historical Background of the Juvenile Justice System

Almost whole of the present Indian history relating to crime and delinquency is tied to the English judicial and legal system. No distinction was made between adult crime and juvenile delinquency in either early English or Indian history. If the youngster was involved in the commission of a criminal act, he was tried in an adult court and was usually subjected to the same criterion for processing and determining guilt. There were "young criminals" but no "delinquent children". Thus, juvenile justice in its present form is a twentieth century's baby.

However, the legal history of handling of children is characterized by a comparatively early recognition and gradual development of a distinction in the disposition of young and adult offenders, chiefly because of minority considerations. Humanitarian and religious features in the handling of juvenile offenders can also be identified by a close examination of legal and non-legal literature of almost all the communities.

(a) In Ancient India

Before the Britishers politically settled in Indian Sub-continent after the battle of Buxsur and battle of Plassay, both the Hindu and Muslim customary laws were in operation in India, although criminal law was almost totally based upon the religious notions of the Muslims. We do not have any specific reference to the juvenile delinquency or child offenders in the legal system in operation immediately before the introduction of English legal system in India. However, some traces of preferential treatment concerning the children can be found in early Hindu ethical codes:

A parent should not administer any punishment for any offence to a child who is under five years of age; children of such tender age should be nursed and educated with love and affection only. After the age of five, punishment may be given in some suitable form, such as physical chastisement or rebuke by the parents. Towards the later half of childhood, however, punishment should be gradually withdrawn and replaced by advice. From the age of 16 years upward sons and daughters should be treated as friends by the parents.

Similarly regarding punishment to some specific categories, including children, a comparatively lenient attitude was shown in ancient Hindu codes. Manu prescribed simple whipping or rebuke for insane, women, infants, the 88 poor and the sick. The Matsya Purana granted concessions for the old and 89 invalid, pregnant woman and children in fixing punishments.

Yajanavalkya in the same way repeated that before inflicting any punishment strength, age, time and place should be taken into consideration. The Mahabharata emphasised that until a boy reached fourteen years he should not be considered sinner even if he committed a sin. Kautilya also favoured exemption to children. These measures reserved for child misconduct were based upon corrective and reformatory philosophy.

Many of the salient features of ancient Indian legal system were lost for a few thousand years following the decline of Hindu era. Certain political developments including the invasion of India by Muslims brought about a total change in the concept of justice, and law and justice became subserviant to Muslim religious philosophy.

But it is to feudal England and the English legal system that the present Indian judicial system, including juvenile justice system, must trace its heritage.

(b) In Pre-Roman and Greek Law

In Pre-Roman and Greek Law some fragmentary references to the handling of juvenile offenders can be pointed out. Of course, these references are not comparable, in their contents and application, to the prevailing approach towards minors on legal and social matters. The relationship between children and their parents is touched upon both in the Code of Hammurabi and in the Mosaic Code. They later stipulated severe punishment, including death, for a child who broke the commandment to honour his parents. In Rabbinic Law we seem to meet the conception of discernment for the first time in the observation that a child nine years and one day old would not be sentenced to death for a capital crime because it was exclusively presumed that "child has no discretion".

(c) In Early Chinese Law

In early Chinese Law also some distinction was maintained, based upon age, for the purpose of penal liability. An offender under seven years of age was completely exempt from punishment. Offenders between seven and ten were recommended for the Emperor's clemency and in the case of non-capital offences an offender between ten and fifteen were subjected to fine only.

(d) In Roman Law

So far Roman Law is concerned there are many detailed reference in connection with the legal position and capacity of the juveniles pertaining to civil rights and liabilities. But in the area of criminal law the legal provisions are scanty and not very specific in nature and contents. In the Twelve Tables we can find two references in two sections dealing with the distinction between the handling of juvenile and adult offenders. The difference was probably due to the distinction recognized by the law of the Twelve Tables - between intentional and unintentional violation 100 of legal norms.

In cases of juveniles lenient consequences usually followed in comparison to adults. Although the Roman Law(Twelve Tables) did not recognize the concept of absolute irresponsibility from crime on the part of the juveniles but gradually the idea of considering juveniles under puberty gained acceptance.

According to Labeo and Ulpianus there was no criminal liability for any damage done by a child, and in cases of those juveniles who had not obtained puberty, liability was conditioned with requirements of sufficient intelligence to commit a legal offence. Justinian observes "my decision is, since theft depends upon intent that one under the age of puberty is liable only in case he is near puberty and, for that reason, knows that he is doing wrong". In this way the Roman Law on criminal responsibility between infancy and puberty came to depend on a combination of three factors: chronological age and its proximity to either infancy or puberty; nature 106 of the offence; and mental capacity of the offender'.

(e) In German Law

In the medieval German Law the approach towards children, both in civil and criminal law, differed more or less not only from state to state but also from time to time. Various upper age limits of penal minority were recognised in different states which ranged from 7 to 15 years. However, penal minority did not necessarily mean exemption from all sanctions of 108 punitive or compensatory nature. The basis of exemption of children from punishment was their presumed incapacity to distinguish between "right and wrong" between "good and evil" in other words their inability to understand the nature of their acts.

(g) In Anglo Saxon and Early English Common Law

During the early Anglo-Saxon period some (fragmentary) isolated instances of criminal responsibility of children and criterion for fixing criminal responsibility of children can be traced. Children of ten and twelve years were ordinarily held responsible for theft and robbery depending upon the period of rule of a particular King. Infancy, accordingly, was no defence among the Anglo-Saxons but pardon might be granted to a juvenile under twelve years of age who robbed.

During the period followed by Norman Conquest there was no rule of absolute immunity to children from criminal conduct but pardon and exemption from punishment were being used as a matter of course for juveniles under seven. As a matter of rule there were no definite principles with regard to relationship between the age of an offender and his penal liability and it was discretionary with the judge to decide whether the child is old enough to be punished or not. Later it became settled that juveniles in the sub adolescent period should be presumed not to have attained full power of discrimination and punishment was limited only to those cases which involved malice.

(h) Modern Perspective

It is clear from the perusal of above discussion that differential and comparatively lenient legal approach towards children has always been reflected, in one form or the other, by almost all societies, although by any standards it cannot be compared with the modem concern and approach towards the problem of juvenile delinquency and treatment of young offenders.

(i) Development in England

In English which can rightly be described as a mother of present Indian legal system, the rules relating to the age of relative and absolute immunity from criminal responsibility (7 years and 14 years) were adopted as early as the 17th century and have been upheld since then. (With a modest change in 1933 when the maximum penal age of 7 was raised to 8, and again in 1963, it was raised to 10 years.) Inspite of these statutory provisions for a differential treatment for children, the punishment meted out to young offenders was often very severe and disproportionate to their age and level of maturity. There are instances of death sentences passed on children of eight, even for petty thefts and flocking of thousands of young children to jails along 119 m, with hardened adult prisoners. These circumstances- and mal-treatment destined for the young offenders in jails moved certain socially spirited individuals to voice for refine in the administration of criminal justice to the young.

It was due to the efforts of individuals like Elizabeth Fry and Mary Carpenter, to mention a few; that led to the establishment of Reformatory School for young offenders under the Reformatory School Act of 1854 and 1855. Industrial School Act of 1857 was passed few years later for neglected children who might turn into delinquents. Then followed the chain of many statutory enactments in the latter half of the 19th century, introducing further improvements in the existing statutes. Of these some most important are Reformatory School Acts of 1866, 1872 1891,1893 and The Industrial School Act of 1866, 1879, 1880, 1891.

Another personality, who contributed towards better treatment for the juvenile offenders at the hands of law, was Sir William Harcourt. He, for his efforts and support for a protective treatment to the young offenders, was relentlessly attacked by Press and the Queen, but he ultimately succeeded in the abolition of imprisonment as a preliminary condition for going to a Reformatory School in 1899. Thus the reformatory movement was given statutory recognition and strengthened further by the establishment of first juvenile court in England in 1905, although the legal provision for juvenile courts throughout the country was made by the Children Act of 1908. The concept of juvenile court as a separate jurisdictional agency for dealing with juvenile offenders was relatively new in the 19th century and was preceded by certain developments in the area of reformative philosophy towards young children. The innovative use of probation as a most common method of non-institutional treatment was one of them. Besides this, as has already been noted, correctional facilities for juveniles too were a new idea in the later half of the 19th century as introduced in England and many other countries.

The idea of special and protective treatment to juveniles is a British legacy in India and was introduced during the British Rule.

References

1. Russ Ver Steeg "The Essentials of Greek and Roman Law" , Carolina Academic Press, 2010, Durham.
2. Walter O. Weyrauch, "Gypsy Law- Romani Legal Traditions

and Culture", University of California Press, 2001, Berkeley and Los Angeles.

3. Bret Hinsch, "Women in early imperial China"; 2nd edition; Rowman&Littlefield Publishers, Plymouth 2011.

4. John Gillen, The Age of Criminal Responsibility: "The Frontier between Care and Justice" in "Child Care in Practice", Vol. 12.

5. Bala et al., Juvenile justice systems, an international comparison of problems and solutions, 2002.

6

Development of Juvenile Justice System in India

The Law in India, following British precedents, has developed from the purely primitive and retaliatory approach of the rigid criminal courts towards a gradual acceptance of the humanitarian concept of re-education and protection of "the child in need" as a ward of the state. The march of civilization from the age of foregone jurisprudence of retributive and deterrent justice to rehabilitative, individualized, and scientific justice, as reflected by the present juvenile justice system(at least in the statute books) is not sudden development but a slow and steady progress in the field of criminal jurisprudence. Now, the Goddess of justice has not only unfolded the cloth traditionally tied around its eyes from the time immemorial, buthas also developed many legal and extra-legal instrumentalities to look beyond the crime and the criminal, in order to meet the demands of ever increasing individualized justice. Pre-sentence reports, social inquiry report, age, chance to reform(probation, suspended sentence, parole etc.) are some of the concepts which are now having legal recognition, and can be traced in the historical perspective for their roots and development almost in all legal system.

The first legislative measure in India reflective of rehabilitative philosophy towards children, though incidentally, was the Apprentices Act of 1850(the Act has since been repealed by the Apprentices, Act 1961 which does not contain any such provision). Primarily this Act was with the purpose of regulating the relations between employers and employees. But it also provided for the placement with the employer of such child, between the ages of ten and eighteen years, who had been held guilty of committing a petty offence or who was a destitute. Such child could be committed as apprentices to the employers for training. The Magistrate who could commit the child under the Act was also having the supervisory powers for controlling the relationship between the child apprentice and the employer and used to act as guardian of such child. The provision in the Act was with the underlying idea of properly channelizing the misdirected energies of a juvenile towards the learning of some trade or craft in order to equip him with proper training for earning honest living.

Though enacted with the best of motives the Act failed in its objectives because of some Inherent defects in its framework. Neither it was obligatory for the Magistrate to entrust the child for apprenticeship with the employer nor was the employer under any legal obligation to accept the child even if offered for placement by the magistrate. Also, the magistracy trained in the dogmatic theories did not care to make use of these ameliorating provisions.

The major development, making the beginning of differential treatment in India in favour of the child, was the passing of two basic enactments in the field of criminal justice. Indian Penal Code 1860 and Criminal Procedure

Code 1861 (later on amended in 1884, 1898, and 1973) are the two important statutes which not only codified substantive and procedural laws(criminal) in India but also made a new beginning in the administration of criminal justice by introducing clarity and uniformity in its(criminal law) contents and application.

The Indian Penal Code(Act XLV, of I860) exempts all children under the age of seven from criminal responsibility. It also exempts from all penal in responsibility, children between seven and twelve, who have not attained sufficient maturity of understanding the nature and consequences of his act. The Criminal Procedure Code was enacted in 1861 and later amended in 1884 and 1898. Sections 29-B and 562 of the Code related to the treatment of young children. These sections of the code carried with them the lofty ideals of "social justice" and "reformative philosophy" and thus made the beginning of a progressive approach towards young offenders in the field of procedural law. Section 29-B provided for the trial of any person under 15 years of age for any offence not punishable with death or transportation by a District Magistrate or any magistrate empowered under the Reformatory Schools Act, 1897. This section restricted the jurisdiction of ordinary courts in the trial of juvenile offenders. Section 399 provided that when any person v under the age of 15 years was sentenced by any criminal court to imprisonment for any offence, the court might direct that such person instead of being imprisoned in a ordinary jail, should be confined to any reformatory established by the State Government as a fit place for confinement in which there were means of suitable discipline and training in some branch of useful industry.

Section 562 also made a specific provision for offenders under the age of 21 years for release on probation of good conduct, under certain conditions, instead of sentencing such person to imprisonment. The provision thus provided a fair chance to the young offender to reform himself. Unfortunately this provision has not been liberally used because of the vindictive nature of the police as well as the non-positive attitude of the judiciary.

In chronological order the next major development that was directly and solely devoted towards the treatment and socialization of juvenile offenders without undergoing the rigorous pangs of imprisonment, was the Reformatory Schools Act of 1897. It was an all India measure, which remained in operation in all those States which were having no Children Act. The Act deals with delinquent boys under 16 years of age in Bombay State and under fifteen years elsewhere. The Act made a detailed provision for the setting up and management of Reformatory Schools; a distinctive machinery with the spirit of reformation of youthful offenders. Under the Act "a youthful offender" means boy who has been convicted of any offence punishable with transportation or imprisonment and who at the timeof such conviction was under the age of fifteen years. Such youthful offender, at the discretion of sentencing court, could be sent to a reformatory school instead of jail. The Act also provided for the licencing out of boys over fourteen years of age if suitable employment could be found for him.

In the history of juvenile justice in India, the Reformatory School Act was a landmark development, though it covered only post-sentence juvenile justice. Despite the fact that the working of reformatory schools was punitive in nature, it was an appreciable advance in the field of juvenile legislation. It opened a new era towards the establishment of separate correctional facilities for young offenders in India. Another allied development in supplementing the Reformatory Schools Act was the Criminal Tribes Amendment Act, 1897, which has a very limited operation. It provided for the establishment of industrial, agricultural and reformatory schools for children, between the age of four and eighteen years, of members of any notified criminal tribe. The local government, under the Act, was empowered to remove such children from Criminal tribes settlements and place them in a reformatory under the charge of a superintendent.

To sum up, the characteristic feature of the period before 1919 was limited only to one aspect of the juvenile justice system i.e., avoiding the juvenile offenders from being sent to jail and reformation through imparting training while in custodial facility. All these legislative measures, besides giving a legal recognition in clear terms to the special status and rights of the child offenders, were insulated with the embryonic ideals of preferential and socialized treatment of youthful offenders. These legislative measures served as the basis for the further development of child welfare legislation in India and ultimately culminated in the establishment of special courts for the socially handicapped young delinquents. And that is the beginning of an era of new philosophy which later on came to be known by a specific term, "Juvenile justice system". It(system) not only embraces within its fold the already operative fragmentary variables of juvenile justice (like Probation services, separate correctional facilitiesbut also formally launched the apex body of the system - juvenile court. This made the beginning of major departure from the traditional penal approach to juvenile offenders.

The landmark development in the area of juvenile justice system was the Report of the Indian Jails Committee(1919-20). The Committee strongly recommended major correctional reforms in the administration of criminal justice in general and specific observations were made for toning up the juvenile justice system in India. The Report pointed out that the child was mainly a product of environment in which he happens to be or is forced to be. He has a natural right for fresh opportunities to grow and live under more congenial conditions. The Committee observed that the juvenile and youthful offender was more amenable to re-education and treatment since his attitude not being fixed can be more conveniently changed.

The committee made many recommendations directly dealing with the improvement in the working of juvenile justice delivery system. Some of the recommendations are:

(a) The Committee favoured separate trial and treatment of youthful offenders. It observed the commitment to a prison of children and young persons, whether after conviction or while on remand or under trial, is contrary to public policy and sentences of imprisonment should, in cases of children and young persons, be made illegal.

(b) Liberal use of non-institutional treatment was other recommendation of the committee. The Report read:"It is often considered to leave a child offender to his parents, if the home is at all a decent one.

(c) The committee favoured the creation of a separate children's court for the hearing of all cases against children and young persons and adoption of informal and elastic procedure in such courts

(d) Specially trained Magistrates to deal with the cases of children and young persons was another observation of the committee. The Report did not favour the appointment of one Magistrate for a large jurisdiction as it causes more harm than good because of resultant inconvenience to children because of long distance from their homes

(e) A pre-sentence report was another main recommendation of the Committee. In order to arrive at a decision the magistrate should have before him information regarding child's home his habits and circumstances, which led him into crime. Before a final order is made there should be an adjournment for the collection of such information about the child offender. In the meanwhile, the child should be released i on bail or sent to a remand home but in no case he should be sent to jail.

(f) Institution of Probation system and its extensive use both for collecting information regarding children and also to supervise them after release was another major recommendation of the Committee.

In view of the spate of legislation that immediately followed the submission of Jail Committee's Report(1919-20), it can be said that this Report made a significant contribution in the introduction and development of juvenile justice system in India. Madras Children Act, 1920 was the first legislative in this direction in point of time, though it took almost two decades(19 years) to establish a juvenile Court under the Madras Children Act,1920. On the other hand in Bengal the juvenile court was established in Calcutta eight years ahead of passing the Bengal Children Act, 1922.

Next to follow was Bombay Children Act 1924. All these Children Acts were by and large corresponding to Children Act 166 of 1908 of England. All these provincial Acts made provisions for juvenile courts, probation services and institutional treatment in order to secure the ends of juvenile justice. No difference was made between delinquent and neglected children so for their legal processing, care, protection and rehabilitation under the Children Acts was concerned.

It was only in response to the impact of many decisions of the Apex Court concerning the rights of prisoners specially the child delinquents that a serious thought to this aspect of social welfare developed and some other states passed/ enforced Children Acts with some seriousness. This is pertinent from the thought provoking observation of Justice V.R. Krishna Iyer in the case of Inder Singh v. Delhi Admn. The judge observed:

> *"Instead of bolting young men behind the high walls of a prison and forgetting about them, humanising influences must be brought to bear upon them so that a better sense of responsibility, a kindlier attitude, behavioural maturity and values of good life may be generated under controlled conditions."*

Though the response was not very encouraging at the administrative level which adopted a luke-warm approach towards the establishment of infrastructure essential for providing necessary support-system to the juvenile.

References

1. Chatterjee S.K; Offences against children and juvenile offence (central law publications, Allahabad, 2nd edition, 2016, 407.
2. Muller, M.F. (6). The Laws of Manu. Oxford: Clarendon Press
3. Unnithan, N. Prabha (2013). Crime and Justice in India; in Kethineni Sesha & Braithwaite Jeremy (eds.), Towards a Compliance Model: The Indian Supreme Court and the Attempted Revolution in Child Rights. New Delhi: Sage Publications.
4. Chatterjee, G. „The Reformation of Neglected and Delinquent Children in British Raj: An Historical Overview , in Material for National Workshop on Neglected Children; by Prayas, Shramik Vidyapeeth and Delhi School of Social Work, New Delhi.
5. Saibaba, Anuradha. Juvenile Justice: Critically Juxtaposing the Models in India and Singapore (Working Paper Series No. 28), September 2012, Asian Law Institute.

7

Understanding The Juvenile Justice Act

Before getting involved in the sophisticated philosophical complexities of juvenile justice system, it is worthwhile to try and understand what the term "System" and "Justice" means in the context of administration of criminal justice to juveniles.

(a) What Is System?

The following general comment about "system" seems appropriate in the juvenile justice background: Any time we assemble people and things and arrange for them to go about performing a task, we have designed a system.lt may be an abysmally inferior system. The system's engineering may be rated as of lawofequality, in some instances hardly recognizable as engineering. But it is still a system.

Directly in relation to juvenile justice system, Alan Coffey describes that "a system can be thought of as a means of organising and processing input in order to attain specific ends. Input in the case of juvenile justice, is certain law violators defined as delinquents; process is the activities of police, probation, juvenile court and juvenile corrections; and output is the collective(and, therefore, systematically related) success of these processes.

In the simplest terminology, a system can be stated as an arrangement of certain things in systematic manner with the primary purpose of attaining certain pre-desired objectives through its working. In the system designing efforts are concentrated upon the maximum output with minimum cost and low wastage. The level of achievement, may be high or low, in terms of the efficiency of any system's working, can be useful only in its rating as a system - very good, good, bad, but cannot be concluded to deny it the status of a system in case of its poor output. Certainly in such a situation a system needs improvement, innovation or total change. But so long it operates; it will continue to be known as a system. In the context of juvenile justice a system can be defined as "legal infrastructure designed for the purpose of transmitting "justice" in the cases involving juvenile offenders". It includes all the related agencies through which it operates, starting from the police organization, including juvenile courts, juvenile welfare boards, probation services and institutional and non-institutional correctional setup.

Juvenile justice system has been described by commentators "as being so unsystematic as to be a non-system"; a "poorly functioning system that has suffered from lack of attention to system design and engineering"; "too much fragmented in operation" in spite of all the functional and philosophical shortcomings the juvenile justice system continues to be known as a system, and rightly so. It begins with and includes the primary system designer's (legislature) legal framework (Juvenile Acts and other institutional agencies) and subsequently its renovator's(courts) improvements and innovations through judicial pronouncements. Defective design-setting or operational problems or absence of a single system-manager cannot be considered as sufficient justifications to treat juvenile justice system as a non-system. At the most we can describe it as poorly co-ordinated system with lot of scope for improvement in its design and out-put efficiency.

(b) What is Justice?

Justice has been perhaps the most frequently used term in legal literature of the present as well as of the ancient societies. It has been described by various names(like Dharma in the ancient India) and has been interpreted in a different manner by different societies and at different times. Even in the same society different people interpret the term from different angles with altogether different meanings in similar and not so similar situations.

The sense, in which the term "justice" has been explained in the context of juvenile justice, emphasises the injustice of letting children "get away" with the damage they cause to the society. The stress here is protection of the interests of the society from the ever increasing juvenile crime by orientation of the whole juvenile justice process from that angle. This is the sense most frequently used by the police# magistrates and all those who are not persuaded by "liberal" and "reformative" views of what should be done with young offenders. The supporters of this approach also include the writers who describe juvenile justice system as full of "structural and procedural faults" which has failed to provide desired output.

We can come to the conclusion that "justice" besides being an attempt at maintenance of order has much wider scope and implications, specially in its application to young offenders. It is a fundamental value in itself and most constructive means of creating a better society. On one hand order demands that the offender should be dealt in a manner appropriate to the protection of the society and consolatory to the feelings of the victim. On the other hand civilized and better social living demands protective and reformative approach in dealing with juvenile offenders. In each case it is taken as "justice" by different sections of the society. This apparent conflict between "justice" in the sense of order and justice in the sense of "social welfare" must be balanced in order to formulate an efficient juvenile justice delivery system. Since social situations provoke new thoughts, leading to the establishment of more meaningful and effective system in almost every field of life, so juvenile justice system must always keep its doors open to new thoughts in order to reach at the desired output level. In that manner "justice" is a progressive and living concept. It must strive for a better and more civilized society without losing its touch with the prevalent social realities.

(c) Juvenile Justice System

As a natural response to the comprehensive and broad based meaning of the terms "system", "justice" and "juvenile delinquency", the juvenile justice system has emcompassed ideals of care, concern treatment and rehabilitation, as its predominant theme for all categories of socially handicapped children - offender delinquents and non-offender delinquents. Thus "the juvenile justice system implies the administration of laws - by judicial or administrative authorities - related not only to persons under 21 years of age who are alleged or found to have committed crime or to have shown other delinquent (anti-social) behaviour, but also pertaining to neglected and dependent children in need of care and protection.

For the administration and execution of these lofty aims and objectives, juvenile justice embodies various branches, each of which may be a special, more or less, integral part of a particular principal system of criminal or social justice. In other words}various procedural and treatment branches of a particular national system of juvenile justice(juvenile court, juvenile corrections, juvenile welfare Boards, juvenile police Bureau and juvenile probation services) have the ultimate purpose to provide support, care, training to persons on the exclusive basis of their social and personal needs with the welfare of the child always as a primary goal. The system has its basis in the protective and assisting, "parens patrae" philosophy which is the main internal characteristic of all institutions, laws and procedures providing for differential handling of juveniles falling under its jurisdictional scope -be they neglected or delinquent (offender). Apparently, from philosophical angle, the juvenile justice system is a unitary process, a combination of many variables with a common goal of rehabilitation and reintegration of the delinquent juvenile without endangering the safety of the society.

The process begins with the primary law enforcement agency's (police) first contact with the deviant youth and passes through many other variables like juvenile court/ Welfare Board, probation service and may intimately end up with institutionalized or non-institutionalized treatment. In that manner the whole process is moved at and guided by the dual aims, maximum welfare of the child in trouble with the mini mum sacrifice of social safety - a task which cannot be achieved to every body's satisfaction.

In the words of Dr. Hira Singh, "Juvenile justice system represents an organised effort on the part of the State to restore for children in situations of social maladjustment, their basic rights to grow and develop as healthy individuals. While the concept of juvenile justice, in its wider perspective, implies the provision of the welfare and well-being of all the children in need of care and protection, the formal system of juvenile justice actually deals with those who are already in conflict with law or are likely to be so for various reasons"

From the above observation and its implications we can conclude that juvenile justice system means and includes within its fold all those legal and extra-legal processes methods, institutions, individuals, who work/operate towards the end of juvenile justice philosophy.

References

1. Chakraborty, Tapan. (2002). Delinquency and Juvenile Justice System in India in John A. Winterdyk (ed.), The Juvenile Justice Systems: International Perspectives, 2nd ed., Toronto: Canadian Scholars' Press.
2. Hartjen, A. Clayton & Kethineni, Sesha (1996). Comparative Delinquency India and the United States, New York & London: Garland Publishing
3. Bajpai, G.S. (2006). 'Making it Work: Juvenile Justice in India', Paper presented at the National Seminar on Care & Protection of Disadvantaged Children in Urban India
4. 'Causes and Consequences of Juvenile Delinquency in India', Recent Research in Science and Technology 2013
5. Ved Kumari (2004), The Juvenile Justice in India: From Welfare to Rights, New Delhi: Oxford University Press.

8

Juvnile Justice System Versus Criminal Justice System

In order to infuse further clarity in the concept of juvenile justice as a "system", it is most appropriate to distinguish the juvenile justice system from the criminal justice system, which is fast coming up as a separate system.

The philosophy and the underlying idea behind the juvenile justice system present a radical departure from the criminal court philosophy of retributive justice and "an eye to eye". Although basic functional approach of both the systems is the same, and follows same sequence of procedural formalities for the flowof justice: Firstly, there is violation of certain accepted social norm leading to contact with the law enforcement agency in the form of apprehension. Then it follows similar judicial process of investigation, inquiry and trial, ultimately resulting into guilty or not guilty and in case of unfavourable disposition, institutional or non-institutional correctional efforts follow. Both justice systems use the same basic tone though literal terminology used differs considerably without much change of intent involved in their use. Even then there is a marked difference in the functioning and philosophy of two systems.

The significant difference between the two is the degree of emphasis on treatment and rehabilitation option, with juvenile justice system attaching more attention to individualized treatment and welfare of the young offender. The age old supposition that juveniles are more malleable than adults still pervades the juvenile justice process and encourages a greater emphasis on correctional efforts. This fact has been reflected by the careful selection of words with a non-punitive tone in the statutes dealing with children.

Besides the basic philosophy the most significant feature of the juvenile justice system are characterized by distinctive procedures and methods of treatment of children. One of the ways of defining the basic characteristics of the system is to compare the juvenile justice system with the criminal justice system.

Ordinarily, as Tappan has explained, there has been a tendency to do this comparison by contrasting the most favourable picture that can be presented of the juvenile justice system with a most dismal and unrealistic one of the adult criminal court. At present, the actual functional aspect of the juvenile courts is practically devoid of juvenile justice philosophy and hardly even statutory requirements of juvenile laws are met. That way there is not much different between juvenile courts and ordinary criminal courts so for their real practices are concerned.

This question involves two aspects, firstly, what the juvenile justice system is expected to achieve(philosophy) and what structural and procedural framework for that purpose has been created, which is different from the criminal justice system. Secondly, how the juvenile justice system actually operates and how much successful it is to achieve what it is expected to achieve? The first question can be partially answered here by presenting a broad comparison between the two systems. The sustained comparison of what are considered to be fundamental characteristics of juvenile justice and conventional criminal courts should provide an additional understanding of basic juvenile justice philosophy.

One of the fundamental difference between the two systems if they can be called two separate systems, is that criminal justice broadly proclaims and meticulously tries to protect a fundamental right to liberty and ordinarily non-interventionist approach in the life circle of an adult individual is the rule unless it is absolutely necessary otherwise. Conversely, the juvenile justice system is founded on a fundamental duty of the state to provide parental care and protection if for some reason it is not being offered by the natural parents.

Thus juvenile justice system assigns an active and positive role to the state to act as super parents of the child in need, while adult system requires the state to play a passive and negative role in order to confine the adult offender within certain predetermined limits. It means that adults have a fundamental legal right to be free of governmental intervention in their life activities except in certain circumstances. On the other hand children have a fundamental right to receive governmental intervention in their life unless they are being properly cared by their natural parents.

Secondly, strong adversary nature of the criminal court proceedings makes it a battle ground, where "belligerents meet to try their strength". In a war of words between prosecution and the defence in their efforts to prove or disprove the guilt of the accused, the court acts more or less like a referee. The trial is characterised by contentiousness or what has been described as an "adversary combative proceedings".

On the other hand in case of the child offender the "attention of the court is directed primarily towards the understanding the meeting of the child's needs. The purpose of the juvenile court is to see "what he is (juvenile), how he has become what he is, and what could best be done in his interest and in the interest of the state to save him from a downward career". So the approach of the court in the whole process is clinical and its hearing characterised as scientific method of investigation.

Thirdly, the criminal court is guided by the fact of finding whether the accused has committed the alleged offence, and if so, the ascertain punishment appropriate to the gravity of the offence. But in case of proceedings before the juvenile court the object is not limited only to find out whether the child is delinquent or not but goes even beyond that, at all the stages of the proceedings. The court has to find out why he is delinquent and what kind of-treatment shall be necessary to put him on the right track of life circle. The fixing of blame is not considered to be as important as it is in the criminal court. The primary purpose is to find out whether intervention of the social control agencies is necessary and if so what kind of treatment alternative shall be most suitable in the case before the court.

Fourthly, while a criminal trial is public and represents action of the state against the offender; a juvenile court hearing is nearly always private proceeding to which only interested parties may be admitted. Additionally a ring of protection from wide publicity has been provided by prohibiting the publication of names, address of a school or any other particular calculated to lead to the defamation of the child.

In criminal trial strict evidentiary rules are adhered to in the conduct of proceedings by the courts and sharp actions and reactions from prosecution and defence follow throughout the recording of evidence. Thus the court plays a very passive role and meticulously follow the prescribed procedural rules. But in case of the proceedings before the juvenile court lot of flexibility is permitted and the atmosphere is informal and friendly. Although no separate standard of proof is prescribed for the proceedings involving juveniles but in keeping with the object and purpose of the juvenile laws it is generally lower than required in the adult criminal court. The specific conduct is relevant more as symptomatic of a need for the court to bring its healing power to bear than as pre-requisite to exercise jurisdiction. For the selection of appropriate treatment alternative for the child in need, emphasis is placed upon a scientific investigation of social and other factors which induced the child into life of crime.

In view of the strong reaction the public ordinarily has towards criminal and criminality in general and adult crime in particular, deterrent and retributive philosophy still dominates in the determination of the punishment and proportionality between crime and punishment is ordinarily maintained, both at legislative level and judicial dispositional level. But in the cases involving juveniles special consideration is given at both the levels to the specific needs of the child and accordingly same rationality does not prevail in fixing punishment for offences involving young offenders. Death punishment or imprisonment of young offenders is totally forbidden and only in most appropriate cases institutionalized treatment is offered as a last resort only. Thus gravity of the offence, if any, under the penal court seldom bears nexus with the treatment plan offered by juvenile justice system.

In order to effectively achieve the objectives for which juvenile justice system exists, many structural, jurisdictional, procedural and normative changes have been introduced in the administration of criminal justice to the section of the society consisting of young offenders. That way an independent sub-system of criminal justice system is in the making, yet to achieve a full status and recognition. Separate juvenile court, separate probation service, and separate police service, separate correctional facilities are strong moves towards that end.

References

1. Handbook for Advocates working with Children in Conflict with Law in India under The Juvenile Justice (Care and Protection of Children) Act, 2015 & Juvenile Justice (Care and Protection of Children) Model Rules 2016.

2. Sahmey K, Patnaik B. A Study on FactorsUnderlying Juvenile Delinquency and PositiveYouth Development Programs; Department ofHumanities and Social Sciences National Institute of Technology Rourkela-769008, Odisha, India. 2013.

3. Bridges KMB. Factors Contributing to JuvenileDelinquency, 17 Am. nst. Crim. L. Criminol. (1920 Chowdhury IA, Khan MM, Uddin I. Causes and Consequences of Juvenile Delinquency).

4. Arlene Manoharan and Swagata Raha, The Juvenile Justice System in India and Children who commit serious offences –Reflection on the Way Forward. Centre for Child and the Law, National Law School University of India, Bangalore.

5. Contribution for the International Colloquium on Juvenile Justice, 16-18 March, 2013, New Delhi

6. United Nations Standard Minimum Rules for the Administration of Juvenile Justice, 1985 (the Beijing Rules) and theUnited Nations Rules for the Protection of Juvenile Deprived of their Liberty.

9

Juvenile Perspective Under The International Regime

There were mainly two different rationales in varied parts of the world for the establishment of a separate system for juveniles: (i) the principle of segregation of children from adult offenders; and (ii) the principle of parens patriae, i.e, the state is responsible for all juveniles requiring care and protection. Gradually, the 'welfare' approach [parens patriae] shifted to the 'rights' approach, which respects the Constitutional and procedural rights of a juvenile. Juvenile justice has since been acknowledged as part of the human rights discourse. A child in conflict with the law should "be treated in a manner consistent with the promotion of the child's sense of dignity and worth, and which reinforces the child's respect for the human rights and fundamental freedoms of others and which takes into account the child's age and the desirability of promoting the child's reintegration and the child's assuming a constructive role in society."

To effectively represent a child in conflict with the law, it is imperative that the lawyer has knowledge about the reasons why a child in conflict with the law is treated differently from an adult, though the offence committed may be similar. Such treatment is not lenient, as many believe - it is age-appropriate.

On the International Platform

Reference is being made to the United Nations international instruments to show that juvenile justice falls within the human rights sphere, and is so acknowledged globally. Such international instruments have been referred to in the preamble of the JJ Act, 2015 as being the reason for re-enactment of juvenile justice legislation.

Some of their clauses are contained in the said Act, and may be relied upon by lawyers to support their arguments. That child offenders should be transformed, and not penalized, was a theory advocated by the first international instrument on children's rights, the Geneva Declaration of the Rights of the Child, 1924. It places a duty on mankind – "the delinquent child must be reclaimed".

In 1985, the United Nations Standard Minimum Rules for the Administration of Juvenile Justice, [the Beijing Rules] spelt out in detail the treatment to be meted to juveniles. It defines "juveniles" as "a child or young person who, under the respective legal systems, may be dealt with for an offence in a manner which is different from an adult". It obligates the adjudicating authority to conduct proceedings in a manner that is "conducive to the best interests of the juvenile and shall be conducted in an atmosphere of understanding, which shall allow the juvenile to participate therein and to express herself or himself freely". It also extends to a juvenile, the procedural safeguards assured to an adult – such as the presumption of innocence, the right to be notified of the charges, the right to remain silent, the right to counsel, the right to the presence of aparent or guardian, the right to confront and cross-examine witnesses andthe right to appeal to a higher authority shall be guaranteed at all stages ofproceedings.

Focus of the Beijing Rules is on rehabilitation of the juvenile, and it stipulates a "variety of disposition orders" as an alternative to imprisonment – such as care, guidance and supervision orders; probation; community service orders; orders to participate in group counseling and similar activities. The Beijing Rules discourage pre-trial and post-trial detention – "Detention pending trial shall be used only as a measure of last resort and for the shortest possible period of time" and "The placement of a juvenile in an institution shall always be a disposition of last resort and for the minimum necessary period."

In 1990, two international instruments regarding juvenile justice were adopted by the United Nations General Assembly - the United Nations Rules forthe Protection of Juveniles Deprived of their Liberty [the Havana Rules] and the United Nations Guidelines for the Prevention of Juvenile Delinquency [the Riyadh Guidelines]. What is of interest in the present discussion are the Havana Rules. The Havana Rules is the first international instrument that defines 'juvenile' in terms of age – "A juvenile is every person under the age of 18". The aim of the juvenile justice system as reflected under the Havana Rules is to "uphold the rights and safety and promote the physical and mental well-being of juveniles."

Furthermore, The Rules are intended to establish minimum standards accepted by the United Nations for the protection of juveniles deprived of their liberty in all forms, consistent with human rights and fundamental freedoms, and with a view to counteracting the detrimental effects of all types of detention and to fostering integration in society.

The Havana Rules also castigates pre-trial detention – "Detention before trial shall be avoided to the extent possible and limited to exceptional circumstances", as also post-trial incarceration – Deprivation of the liberty of a juvenile should be a disposition of last resort and for the minimum necessary period and should be limited to exceptional cases. The length of the sanction should be determined by the judicial authority, without precluding the possibility of his or her early release.

The Convention on the Rights of the Child, 1989, [CRC] is the international treaty on children's rights that India acceded to in 1992. Articles 37 and 40 of the CRC deal with children in conflict with the law. The UNCRC also reiterates that detention "shall be used only as a measure of last resort and for the shortest appropriate period of time". State Parties are mandated to ensure that "every child alleged as or accused of having infringed the penal law", has the following, amongst other, guarantees –be presumed innocent until proven guilty according to law"; "to have legal or other appropriate assistance in the preparation and presentation of his or her defence"; "to have the matter determined without delay by a competent, independent and impartial authority or judicial body in a fair hearing according to law, in the presence of legal or other appropriate assistance".

Legal representation is a crucial and integral part of fair trial. A child in conflict with the law is entitled to be defended by a lawyer. In this respect, the Beijing Rules state, "Throughout the proceedings the juvenile shall have the right to be represented by alegal adviser or to apply for free legal aid where there is provision for such aid in the country." Under the Havana Rules, "Juveniles should have the right of legal counsel and be enabled to apply for free legal aid, where such aid is available, and to communicate regularly with their legal advisers. Privacy and confidentiality shall be ensured for such communications".

The UNCRC also provides for legal assistance to a child in conflict with the law - "Every child deprived of his or her liberty shall have the right to prompt access to legal and other appropriate assistance". General Comment No. 10 [2007]: Children's rights in juvenile justice, too states, The child must be guaranteed legal or other appropriate assistance in the preparation and presentation of his/ her defence. CRC does require that the child be provided with assistance, which is not necessarily under all circumstances legal but it must be appropriate.

The Committee recommends the State parties provide as much as possible for adequate trained legal assistance, such as expert lawyers or paralegal professionals. Prof. Ved Kumari refers to the Report of the Indian Jail Committee 1919-1920 as The aforementioned international instruments may be innovatively relied upon by lawyers representing children in conflict with the law to ensure constitutional and procedural safeguards, including the right to a fair trial / inquiry; child's best interest; release on bail; speedy disposal of inquiry; appropriate rehabilitative measures and community-based disposition orders.

References

1. David S. Tanenhaus, The Elusive Juvenile Court: Its Origins, Practices, and ReInventions, in The Oxford Handbook of Juvenile Crime and Juvenile Justice

2. Paula S. Fass, A Historical Context for the United Nations Convention on the Rights of the Child.

3. Convention on the Rights of the Child, Nov. 20, 1989, 1557 U.N.T.S.

4. U.N. Standard Minimum Rules for the Administration of

Juvenile Justice (The Beijing Rules)

5. 3 Economic and Social Council Res. 1997/30, Guidelines for Action on Children in the Criminal Justice System

6. General Assembly U.N. Guidelines for the Prevention of Juvenile Delinquency (The Riyadh Guidelines).

7. General Assembly U.N. Rules for the Protection of Juveniles Deprived of Their Liberty (The Havana Rules).

8. Elizabeth S. Scott & Laurence Steinberg, Adolescence and the Regulation of Youth Crime.

10

Rights of Children Alleged and Found To Be in Conflict With The Law

The Constitution of India recognizes the unique status of children in many of itsprovisions. Several Articles contained in Part III and Part IV of the Constitution – Fundamental Rights and Directive Principles of State Policy, respectively, – are also applicable to children. The Constitution particularly empowers the State to frame special laws for children under Article 15(3). Specific obligations are placed on the State to ensure that children are protected from exploitation, and receive free and compulsory education. While fundamental rights are enforceable and justiciable, directive principles are non-enforceable, yet provide guidance for good governance.

The Constitution also prohibits traffic in human beings and forced labour, and the employment of children below 14 years in hazardous employment in Articles 23 and 24, respectively. In Article 39 (e) and (f), obligation is cast on the State to ensure that tender age of children is not abused and "children are given opportunities and facilities to develop in a healthy manner and in conditions of freedom and dignity and that childhood and youth are protected against exploitation and against moral and material abandonment." These directive principles are referred to in the Preamble of the JJ Act, 2015 and hold deep significance for children in conflict with the law and would require the State to ensure that they are not stigmatized, isolated, and deprived of rehabilitative services and opportunities.

In addition to the above provisions, the other fundamental rights in the Constitution such as the right to fundamental freedoms (Article 19), the right to freedom of religion (Article 25), etc., apply to them as well.The Supreme Court has, through judicial activism, elevated some directive principles to the status of fundamental rights. The right to education, for instance, was a directive principle that was held to be a constituent of the right to life under Article 21, before Article 21A was introduced.

Role of the Supreme Court in Enhancing Rights of Children in Conflict with the Law

The Supreme Court can be directly approached under Article 32 and the High Court under Article 226, to seek relief for a violation of fundamental rights. In 1986, in Sheela Barse v. Union of India, the Supreme Court's attention was drawn to the large number of children, including children with mental and physical disabilities, who were languishing in jails in different states of the country. The Court expressed its disapproval at this state of affairs, stating that not only was keeping a child in jail illegal, exposure to the baneful influences of jail had the effect of coarsening a child's conscience and alienating him from the society, all of which is also highly detrimental to the development of the child.

Taking note of the dismal conditions in which the

Juvenile Courts were functioning, the Supreme Court recommended the Central Government to enact uniform legislation in force throughout India for the protection of children in conflict with the law. The Juvenile Justice Act, 1986 was enacted pursuant to this, as also to the adoption of the United Nations Standard Minimum Rules for the Administration of Juvenile Justice (Beijing Rules) by the international community.The writ jurisdiction of the Supreme Court and High Courts has been invoked several times to draw attention to the rights violations of children in conflict with the law. For instance, in Court on Its Own Motion v. Dept. of Women and Child Development, the Delhi High Court received a letter pointingout that many times when the accused persons are arrested by the Police and even when they happen to be children, they are lodged in Tihar Jail and subjected to the hardship of the adult criminal justice system. The Court issued directions that when a person suspected to be a child has been lodged in a jail, he/she shall be kept separately from all other prisoners and be produced before the JJB.

The Investigating Officers (IO), while making arrest, should reflect the age of the prisoner arrested in the Arrest Memo. The court also ordered the introduction of "Age Memo" on the line of "Arrest Memo" to facilitate this process. When a young person, appears to be below 18 years of age or where his arrest memo age states his age to be 18-21 years, is arrested and produced before the Magistrate, it will be the duty of the Magistrate also to order ascertainment of age of such a person. The Court also declared that when any police officer receives a complaint that a juvenile has been treated as an adult, he or she should record the statement of such complainant and then to register a DD Entry and cause corrective steps to be taken.

In Sampurna Behura v. Union of India, a case that

was ongoing since 2005, the apex court directed all State Governments to establish authorities under the JJ Act, fill vacancies, train officials, and develop curriculums. The Supreme Court's intervention highlighted the non-existence of key institutions like SCPCRs, CWCs and JJB's, all of which are a prerequisite for the implementation of the JJ Act in several States. Notably, the court through its orders has signified the importance of capacity building of stakeholders, transparency and accountability of State Governments through submission of quarterly reports and training for legal aid lawyers and probation officers.

Article 51(1)(c) of the Indian Constitution directs the State to 'foster respect for international law and treaty obligations.' Article 253 of the Constitution vests theParliament with the power to enact laws to implement treaties ratified by India.

In the case of Vishaka v. State of Rajasthan, the Supreme Court held that, in the absence of domestic law provisions, reliance can be placed on international law as well as international norms if they are not in contravention of any existing domestic law and the Constitution.

India has ratified the International Covenant on Civil and Political Rights, 1966 (ICCPR), the International Covenant on Economic, Social and Cultural Rights, 1966 (ICESCR), the Convention on the Elimination of All Forms of Discrimination Against Women, 1976 (CEDAW), the Convention on the Rights of the Child, 1989 (UNCRC), and the Convention on the Rights of the Persons with Disabilities, 2006 (UNCRPD). Of these instruments, the ICCPR and the UNCRC expressly recognise the rights of children in conflict with the law, including children alleged or found to be in conflict with law.

The United Nations has been active in the development

of international standards on juvenile justice, contained in several instruments, such as, the Standard Minimum Rules for the Administration of Juvenile Justice, 1985 (the Beijing Rules), and the United Nations Rules for the Protection of Juveniles Deprived of their Liberty, 1990 (Havana Rules). The preamble of the JJ Act, 2015 refers to the UNCRC, Beijing Rules, and Havana Rules and "other related international instruments".

This would include instruments such as the United Nations Guidelines for the Prevention of Juvenile Delinquency, 1990, (the Riyadh Guidelines), the Guidelines for Action on Children in the Criminal Justice System, 1997(Vienna Guidelines), etc.The rights of children in conflict with the law under domestic and international human rights law (IHRL) are detailed in the Sections below.

1. Right to Equality and Non-Discrimination

Article 14 of the Indian Constitution encapsulates the right to equality before thelaw and equal protection of laws. Article 15(1) prohibits discrimination on groundsof religion, race, caste, sex or place of birth, and Article 15(3) allows the State to makespecial provisions for children.

The Juvenile Justice (Care and Protection of Children)Act, 2000, which has now been replaced by the JJ Act 2015 were both enacted infurtherance of Articles 15(3), 39, 45 and 47.In the wake of the Delhi gang-rape case of 2012 in which a young woman wasbrutally raped by a gang comprising adults and one child aged 17.5 years, theconstitutionality of the JJ Act, 2000 which allowed all persons below 18 years to bedealt with as children irrespective of the nature of the offence, was challenged. In Salil Bali v. Union of India, the constitutionality of the JJ Act, 2000 was upheld andthe Supreme Court observed:

The essence of the Juvenile Justice (Care and Protection of Children) Act, 2000, and the Rules framed thereunder in 2007, is restorative and not retributive,providing for rehabilitation and re-integration of children in conflict with lawinto mainstream society. The age of eighteen has been fixed on account of theunderstanding of experts in child psychology and behavioural patterns that till such an age the children in conflict with law could still be redeemed andrestored to mainstream society, instead of becoming hardened criminals infuture.

The Supreme Court, in many instances, has been very vocal regarding the need toprotect child rights particularly with regard to their special vulnerable status. In Salil Bali v. Union of India, the Supreme Court held that "children are amongst the most vulnerable Sections in any society. They represent almost one-third of theworld's population, and unless they are provided with proper opportunities, the opportunity of making them grow into responsible citizens of tomorrow will slipout of the hands of the present generation."

Children alleged or found to be in conflict with the law should not be discriminated against "on any grounds including sex, caste, religion, ethnicity, place of birth ordisability and equality of access, opportunity and shall be provided to every child." Further, the principle of fresh start under Section 3(xiv), JJ Act, 2015, which requires that "All past records of any child under the Juvenile Justice system should be erased except in special circumstances", also flows from the principle of equalityand non-discrimination as it is premised on the equal treatment of all personsirrespective of their involvement in the juvenile justice system. A child who hascommitted an offence and has been dealt with under the JJ Act will also not sufferdisqualifications attached to convictions under Section 24(1), JJ Act, 2015.

However, a child who is above 16 years, and found to be in conflict with the law bythe Children's Court for a heinous offence after trial as an adult, will not enjoy thisprotection. It can also be argued that the right to equality and non-discrimination would notallow children to be treated disadvantageously based on the nature of the offenceand thus the transfer system provided under the JJ Act, 2015 violates the right toequality and non-discrimination. Further, the retention of the records of childrenwho have been convicted by the Children's Court after being tried as an adultwould violate the right to equality and non-discrimination.

2. Privilege against self-incrimination

Article 20(3) of the Constitution recognizes the privilege against self-incrimination and prohibits compelling an accused person to be a witness against himself. Article40(2)(b)(ii), UNCRC recognizes the right of a child in conflict with the law to not "be compelled to give testimony or to confess guilt". According to the CRC, the term "compelled" should not be narrowly construed to mean only physical force :

The age of the child, the child's development, the length of the interrogation, the child's lack of understanding, the fear of unknown consequences or of a suggested possibility of imprisonment may lead him/her to a confession that is not true. That may become even more likely if rewards are promised such as: "You can go home as soon as you have given us the true story", or lighter sanctions or release are promised.

The Supreme Court has held that "the expression "to be witness against himself" in Article 20(3) of the Constitution "means more than the court process" and includes "[any giving of evidence, any furnishing of information, if likely to have an incriminating impact ensures the description of being witness against himself."

The right against self-incrimination covers every stage where information is furnished and material is collected and the protection extends to any person accused of an offence. Children alleged to be in conflict with law are thus entitled to the right against self-incrimination at all stages including the preliminary assessment.

Rule 8(3)(iii), JJ MR safeguards the constitutional privilege against self- incrimination and prohibits the police from compelling a child to confess guilt and states that a parent or guardian may be present during the police interview. Further, the child cannot be asked to sign any statement. Rule 7.1, Beijing Rules, recognizes the right of juveniles to remain silent, the right to counsel, and the right to presence of a parent or guardian, as basic procedural safeguards, regarded as essential for a"fair and just trial" under various international human rights instruments.

The CRC has also emphasized the importance of ensuring the child's access to a legal or appropriate representative and the presence of a parent or guardian during the questioning. It emphasized an "independent scrutiny of the methods of interrogation to ensure that the evidence is voluntary and not coerced, given the totality of the circumstances, and is reliable." It stated that the following aspects should be considered by a judicial body assessing the voluntary nature and reliability of a child's confession: "age of the child, the length of custody and interrogation, and the presence of legal or other counsel, parent(s), or independent representatives of the child."

An advocate representing a child alleged to be in conflict with the law should explain the privilege to the child and that it is applicable at all stages of the legal process.

The implications of sharing incriminating information about the offence and the child's involvement should be communicated to the child. For instance, information about the manner in which an offence was committed with a psychologist for the purpose of a preliminary assessment could be used to transfer the child to the Children's Court for trial as an adult. This privilege can be invoked, directly or through a legal representative, during the preliminary assessment, even though "preliminary assessment is not a trial" because of its extension to all processes.

Although the term "may" is used with respect to the presence of the child's parent or guardian during a police interview under Rule 8(3)(v), JJ Model Rules, 2016, it could be argued that it would be procedurally unfair to interview a child in the absence of a supportive adult or legal representative. A person below 18 years may not have the developmental maturity to withstand police interrogation and may noteven know that a lawyer could be requested for or the presence of the parent or guardian can be demanded.

3. Right to consult a lawyer and to legal aid

Article 22(1) of the Constitution entitles an arrested person to consult with a lawyer and to be defended by a lawyer of his choice. Further, Article 39-A of the Constitution requires the State to provide free legal aid to ensure that citizens are not prevented from accessing the legal system due to economic or other disabilities.

Children alleged to be in conflict with the law have a right to be heard in all legal and judicial proceedings and free legal aid should be made available to them if they are unable to afford legal representation.

The JJ Act, 2015 and JJ Model Rules, 2016, recognize the right of children in conflict with the law to legal aid. It is the JJB's responsibility to ensure the availability of legal aid through legal services institutions. It should ensure that the LPO in the DCPU and the SLSA or DLSA provide free legal services to the child if the child does not already have an advocate representing him. It is also the duty of the police to inform the DLSA for providing free legal aid to the child.

Under Article 14(3)(d), ICCPR every accused has a right "to defend himself in person or through legal assistance of his own choosing; to be informed, if he does not have legal assistance, of this right; and to have legal assistance assigned to him, in any case where the interests of justice so require, and without payment by him in any such case if he does not have sufficient means to pay for it."

Article 14(3)(b), ICCPR stipulates "adequate time and facilities for the preparation of his defenceand to communicate with counsel of his own choosing" as a minimum guarantee. Article 39(d), UNCRC entitles children deprived of liberty to "prompt access to legal and other appropriate assistance " and "legal or other appropriate assistance in the preparation and presentation of his or her defence".

The "right to counsel" and "free legal aid" is also recognized under the Beijing Rules and the Havana Rules. The Basic Principles on the Role of Lawyers recognize the important role played by lawyers in the administration of justice, the right of person to seek a lawyer of their choice during criminal proceedings, free legal aid, and the duty ofthe government to ensure that prompt access to a lawyer is ensured and in any case not later than 48 hours of the arrest or detention.

The CRC has highlighted the implication of the ICCPR and UNCRC provisions related to legal representation: the child and his/her assistant must have adequate time and facilities for the preparation of his/her defence. Communications between the child and his/her assistance, either in writing or orally, should take place under such conditions that the confidentiality of such communications is fully respected in accordance with the guarantee provided for in article 40 (2) (b) (vii) of CRC, and the right of the child to be protected against interference with his/her privacy and correspondence (art. 16 of CRC).

Article 20(1) of the Constitution prohibits the retrospective application of law in respect of offences. It states, No person shall be convicted of any offence except for violation of the law in force at the time of the commission of the act charged as an offence, nor be subjected to a penalty greater than that which might have been inflicted under the law in force at the time of the commission of the offence.

Section 2(13), JJ Act, 2015, states: "child in conflict with law" means a child who is alleged or found to have committed an offence and who has not completed eighteen years of age on the date of commission of such offence.

Section 5, JJ Act, 2015 pertains to inquiry after a person ceases to be 18 years of age. It states, Where an inquiry has been initiated in respect of any child under this Act, and during the course of such inquiry, the child completes the age of eighteen years, then, notwithstanding anything contained in this Act or in any other Access to the child client, especially if the child is being detained in the OH or the Place of Safety, is necessary for effective legal representation. An advocate representing the child should ensure that sufficient time is allowed by the staff of the OH for communication with the child in private.

4. Non-retroactive juvenile justice

Article 20(1) of the Constitution prohibits the

retrospective application of law inrespect of offences. It states,

No person shall be convicted of any offence except for violation of the law in force at the time of the commission of the act charged as an offence, nor be subjected to a penalty greater than that which might have been inflicted under the law in force at the time of the commission of the offence.

Section 2(13), JJ Act, 2015, states: "child in conflict with law" means a child who is alleged or found to have committed an offence and who has not completed eighteen years of age on the date of commission of such offence.

Section 5, JJ Act, 2015 pertains to inquiry after a person ceases to be 18 years of age. It states, Where an inquiry has been initiated in respect of any child under this Act, and during the course of such inquiry, the child completes the age of eighteen years, then, notwithstanding anything contained in this Act or in any otherlaw for the time being in force, the inquiry may be continued by the Board and orders may be passed in respect of such person as if such person had continued to be a child.

Article 40(2)(a), UNCRC prohibits the retrospective application of juvenile justice and states: "No child shall be alleged as, be accused of, or recognized as having infringed the penal law by reason of acts or omissions that were not prohibited by national or international law at the time they were committed".

There are several procedural safeguards applicable to children in conflict with the law such as production before the JJB within 24 hours, presumption of innocence, information about the apprehension and the charges, etc. Rule 7, Beijing Rules lists the procedural safeguards available to children in conflict with the law: Basic procedural safeguards such as the presumption of innocence, the right to be notified of the charges, the right to remain silent, the right to counsel, the right to the presence of a parent or guardian, the right to confront and cross- examine witnesses and the right to appeal to a higher authority shall be guaranteed at all stages of proceedings.

Article 22(2), Constitution requires the production within 24 hours before a Magistrate of a person arrested or detained in custody. This protection applies in full force to children alleged to be in conflict with the law and the police is duty- bound to produce them before the JJB within 24 hours as per Section 10(1), JJ Act,2015 and Rules 8(3)(i) and 9(1), JJ Model Rules, 2016.

Since the JJ Act, 2015 came into force on 15 January 2016, any child alleged to have committed an offence before the Act came into force should be dealt with in accordance with the JJ Act, 2000. Any provision in the State Rules which provides for the treatment as an adult, of a person apprehended after he completed 18 years for an offence he committed as a child, would violate the constitutional and IHRL prohibition on retrospective application of law related to offences and punishments.

5. Procedural safeguards

There are several procedural safeguards applicable to children in conflict with the law such as production before the JJB within 24 hours, presumption of innocence, information about the apprehension and the charges, etc. Rule 7, Beijing Rules lists the procedural safeguards available to children in conflict with the law: Basic procedural safeguards such as the presumption of innocence, the right to be notified of the charges, the right to remain silent, the right to counsel, the right to the presence of a parent or guardian, the right to confront and cross- examine witnesses and the right to appeal to a higher authority shall be guaranteed at all stages of proceedings.

6. Production before JJB within 24 hours

Article 22(2), Constitution requires the production within 24 hours before a Magistrate of a person arrested or detained in custody. This protection applies in full force to children alleged to be in conflict with the law and the police is duty-bound to produce them before the JJB within 24 hours as per Section 10(1), JJ Act, 2015 and Rules 8(3)(i) and 9(1), JJ Model Rules, 2016.

The CRC has also emphasized the significance of producing a child promptly and the right to legal assistance:Every child deprived of his/her liberty has the right to prompt access to legaland other appropriate assistance, as well as the right to challenge the legality of the deprivation of his/her liberty before a court or other competent, independent and impartial authority, and to a prompt decision on any such action.

Every child arrested and deprived of his/her liberty should be brought before a competent authority to examine the legality of (the continuation of) this deprivation of liberty within 24 hours.Failure to adhere to this essential safeguard is a constitutional violation as well as a breach of the procedures stipulated under the JJ Act, 2015 and JJ Model Rules, 2016.

Advocates should bring this to the attention of the JJB, as it is their duty under Section 8(3)(b) to ensure that "the child's rights are protected throughout the process of apprehending the child, inquiry, aftercare and rehabilitation".

7. Information about charges

Rule 8(3)(iii), JJ MR, 2016, obligates the police to "inform the child promptly and directly of the charges levelled against him through his parent or guardian". Copy of the FIR, if registered, or the police report, should be given to the parent or guardian. The CWPO or the SJPU should inform the parent or guardian of the child about the child's apprehension as soon as possible and direct them to be present when the child is produced before the JJB. The address of the JJB and the time of production should be conveyed to them. Rule 10(5) requires the CWPO to produce witness statements and other documents prepared during investigation within a month of the first production of a child who has completed 16 years and has allegedly committed a heinous offence, a copy of which should be given to the child, parent, or guardian.

Article 40(2)(b)(ii), UNCRC requires the child "to be informed promptly anddirectly of the charges against him or her, and, if appropriate, through his or herparents or legal guardians." The Committee on the Rights of the Child has emphasized that the child should be informed of the charges even in cases that are diverted and that an oral explanation should be provided of the charges as handing over an official document is not sufficient. It stated:

> It is the responsibility of the authorities (e.g. police, prosecutor, judge) to make sure that the child understands each charge brought against him/her.The Committee is of the opinion that the provision of this information to the parents or legal guardians should not be an alternative to communicating this information to the child. It is most appropriate if both the child and the parents or legal guardians receive the information in such a way that they can understand the charge(s) and the possible consequences.

8. Bail as a matter of right

All children alleged to be in conflict with the law are entitled to bail irrespective ofwhether the offence is bailable or non-bailable. Bail can be denied only if the JJB has reasonable grounds to believe that the release would bring the child into association with any known criminal or expose the person to moral, physical or psychological danger or the child's release would defeat the ends of justice.

In Ravi-ul-Islam v. State, in a revision petition, the Delhi High Court considered the denial of bail to a CICL charged under the Narcotic Drugs and Psychotropic Substances Act, 1985 and relying on apex court decisions that considered the JJ Act 2000, a beneficial legislation for the benefit of juveniles held that:

Bail has to be granted to a juvenile, notwithstanding anything contained in the Code of Criminal Procedure, 1973 or any other law for the time being in forcewhich includes the NDPS Act also except for the conditions mentioned inSection 12 itself which, if one examines the same, are also to prevent any damage to the juvenile. The idea behind Section 12 being that the juvenile must be released on bail unless releasing him on bail would be detrimental to him or would entirely defeat the ends of justice.

The gravity of the offence cannot be the sole basis for denying bail. In Ashu Kumar v. State of Uttar Pradesh, the Allahabad High Court was of the view thatthe denial of bail by the JJB because he was charged with rape did not meet the justifications stated in law. Even though the District Probation Officer had opposed the bail application, the High Court opined that his view was not supported by any material which indicated that the child would fall into the company of known criminals, or be subjected to physical or psychological danger or that the grant of bail would defeat the ends of justice. The High Court also held that a bail application of a child in conflict with the law could not be opposed on the ground of gravity of the offence when the parents were willing to reform him.

In Talwinder Singh v. State of Punjab, a child in conflict with the law charged under Section 4, Protection of Children from Sexual Offences Act, 2012 had been denied bail by the JJB because he "may try to tamper with evidence and may also attempt to win over the prosecution witness which would certainly defeats the ends of justice." However, there was no reference to any material that justified these presumptions. Bail was also denied by the Sessions Court based on the gravity of the offence. The Punjab and Haryana High Court held that the orders of the JJB and the Sessions Court were against the spirit of the Act and did not meet any of the three grounds based on which bail can be denied..

9. Presumption of Innocence

The principle of presumption of innocence is recognized as a "fundamental principle" which should be adhered to by the JJB and other agencies while implementing the Act. Section 3(i), JJ Act, 2015 states, "Any child shall be presumed to be an innocent of any mala fide or criminal intent up to the age of eighteen years."

Article 40(2)(b)(i), UNCRC recognizes the right of "every child alleged or accused of having infringed the penal law to be presumed innocent until proven guilty according to law." The Committee on the Rights of the Child in General Comment 55 No.10 (2007) Children's rights in juvenile justice has elaborated on this guarantee and underlined that an understanding of child development is important so that the presumption is applied in practice:

The child has the right to be treated in accordance with this presumption and it is the duty of all public authorities or others involved to refrain from prejudging the outcome of the trial. States parties should provide information about child development to ensure that this presumption of innocence is respected in practice. Due to the lack of understanding of the process, immaturity, fear or other reasons, the child may behave in a suspicious manner, but the authorities must not assume that the child is guilty without proof of guilt beyond any reasonable doubt.

Although the POCSO Act, 2012 provides for the presumption as to certain offences under Section 29 and presumption of culpable mental state under Section 30, these presumptions should not apply in cases involving a child alleged to be in conflict with the law. Section 34(1), POCSO Act unequivocally states that the JJ Act, 2000 will apply if offences under the POCSO Act are committed by a child. The JJ Act, 2000 has been repealed and re-enacted and the JJ Act, 2015 occupies the field related to juvenile justice.

Section 1(4)(i), JJ Act, 2015 states that it is the overriding law withrespect to "apprehension, detention, prosecution, penalty or imprisonment, rehabilitation and social re-integration of children in conflict with law". These provisions read together with Section 3(i), JJ Act, 2015 would imply that a child alleged to have committed an offence under the POCSO Act will be presumed innocent and the presumptions under the POCSO Act will not apply.

Article 40(3), UNCRC mandates States Parties to "promote the establishment of laws, procedures, authorities and institutions specifically applicable to children alleged as, accused of, or recognized as having infringed the penal law..." The JJ Act, 2000 was enacted pursuant to this obligation. The reference to the UNCRC also appears in the Preamble of the JJ Act, 2015. A person who is or was below 18 years at the time of the alleged commission of the offence should be dealt with as a "child in conflict with the law" as per the JJ Act, 2015. Even if a person is apprehended after he attains 18 years, the procedure

An advocate representing a child alleged to have committed an offence under the POCSO Act should resist arguments or attempts to apply the presumption of guilt under the POCSO Act against the child in conflict with the law. An advocate should zealously ensure that the presumption of innocence is respected at every stage. For instance, the JJB's decision to transfer the child to the Children's Court based on the assumption that the child has shown no remorse for the alleged offence would grossly violate the presumption of innocence and should be challenged.

10. Right to be dealt with under the special law for children in conflict with law

Article 40(3), UNCRC mandates States Parties to "promote the establishment oflaws, procedures, authorities and institutions specifically applicable to childrenalleged as, accused of, or recognized as having infringed the penal law..." The JJ Act, 2000 was enacted pursuant to this obligation. The reference to the UNCRC also appears in the Preamble of the JJ Act, 2015. A person who is or was below 18 years at the time of the alleged commission of the offence should be dealt with as a "child in conflict with the law" as per the JJ Act, 2015. Even if a person is apprehended after he attains 18 years, the procedureunder the JJ Act will be followed if the offence was allegedly committed when the person was below 18 years. In recognition of this right, Section 34(1) of the POCSO Act, 2012 provides for all children alleged to have committed offences under the Act to be dealt with as per the JJ Act, 2000.

The JJB is expected to conduct "regular inspection of jails meant for adults to check if any child is lodged in such jails and take immediate measures for transfer of such a child to the observation home". Article 10(1)(b), ICCPR requires "accused juvenile persons" to be separated from adults, while Article 10(1)(c), ICCPR prescribes segregation of juvenile offenders from adults and treatment appropriate to the age and legal status of juveniles. According to Article 14(4), ICCPR, the procedures with respect to juveniles should take into account "their age and the desirability of promoting their rehabilitation."

A plea of juvenility can be raised at any stage and before any court. It can eve be raised after a case has been finally disposed and even after the person has ceased to be a child. For instance, a claim of juvenility can be raised in appeal before the Supreme Court even if it had not been raised at any stage before the trial court or the High Court.

In Abuzar Hossain v. State of West Bengal, the Supreme Court summarized the position on the claim of juvenility in the context of the JJ Act 2000. The following principles stated in the case will also apply to the JJ Act 2015:A claim of juvenility may be raised at any stage even after the final disposal of the case. It may be raised for the first time before this Court as well after the final disposal of the case. The delay in raising the claim of juvenility cannot be a ground for rejection of such claim. The claim of juvenility can be raised in appeal even if not pressed before the trial court and can be raised for the first time before this Court though not pressed before the trial court and in the appeal court.

For making a claim with regard to juvenility after conviction, the claimantmust produce some material which may prima facie satisfy the court that an inquiry into the claim of juvenility is necessary. Initial burden has to be discharged by the person who claims juvenility. The court where the plea of juvenility is raised for the first time should always be guided by the objectives of the 2000 Act and be alive to the position that the beneficent and salutary provisions contained in the 2000 Act are not defeated by the hypertechnical approach and the persons who are entitled to get benefits of the 2000 Act get such benefits. The courts should not be unnecessarily influenced by any general impression that in schools the parents/guardians understate the age of their wards by one or two years for future benefits or that age determination by medical examination is not very precise. The matter should be considered prima facie on the touchstone of preponderance of probability.

11. Right to fair and speedy inquiry

A duty has been cast on the JJB to ensure fair and speedy inquiry under Section 14(5), JJ Act, 2015. In furtherance of this, the JJ Act, 2015 prescribes the time frame within which the inquiry should be completed, and mandates the termination of proceedings in petty offences if the inquiry remains inconclusive after six months.

Under Section 19(1)(i), JJ Act, 2015, the Children's Court is required to adhere to the tenets of a fair trial when trying a child as an adult.

Article 21, Constitution of India, guarantees that a person cannot be "deprived of his life or personal liberty except according to a procedure established by law."

Although couched negatively, its expansive interpretation by the Supreme Court Advocates should acquaint themselves with the age-determination procedures under the JJ Act and take steps to verify the age of their adult clients. A plea of juvenility should be raised at the earliest possible stage to prevent the handling of children as adults and violations of their rights under the juvenile justice system.

12. Right to life

Article 21, Constitution of India, guarantees that a person cannot be "deprived of his life or personal liberty except according to a procedure established by law."

Although couched negatively, its expansive interpretation by the Supreme Courthas led to the recognition of several positive rights such as the right to education, right to food, right to privacy, right to speedy trial, right against handcuffing, and protection against custodial torture.

Further, Articles 46 and 47 require the State to safeguard the educational and economic interests of weaker Sections, and raise the nutritional levels and public health, respectively. For children in conflict with the law living in CCIs, it would imply that their right to education, nutrition, and health should be respected, protected and fulfilled. The minimum standards of care within Child Care Institutions stipulated under Section 53, JJ Act, 2015 and Rules 29-38 of the JJ Model Rules, 2016 pertaining to physical infrastructure, sanitation and hygiene, nutritionand diet scale, medical care, mental health, education, vocational training, and recreational facilities should be ensured to children alleged or found to be in conflict with the law.

13. Right to Education

Article 21-A, of the Constitution recognises the right to free and compulsory education to children between six and fourteen years. Children cannot be deprived of their fundamental right to education because of their detention in a custodial institution like the OH, Place of Safety, or Special Home. There is a constitutional obligation on the State to ensure that children below 14 years in these CCIs are compulsorily provided free education. Further, Article 350-A, a special directive, requires the State to provide adequate facilities for instruction in mother-tongue during primary education to children belonging to linguistic minority groups. This constitutional obligation would also apply to children living in the CCIs.

Children alleged to be in conflict with the law are socially disadvantaged owing to the stigma that immediately attaches to them and their families when an F.I.R. is registered against them. Their right to education is often disrupted when they are detained in a custodial institution or the information about their involvement in an offence spreads.

The right to education of a child alleged and found to be in conflict with the law and between the age of six to fourteen years, that is guaranteed under the Right of Children to Free and Compulsory Education Act, 2009 (RTE Act), will also have to be protected by the JJB. Under the RTE Act, the appropriate government is responsible for ensuring that children belonging to weaker Section or disadvantaged group "are not discriminated against and prevented from pursuing and completing elementary education on any grounds". The RTE Act defines "child belonging to disadvantaged group" to meana child with disability or a child belonging to the Scheduled Caste, the Scheduled Tribe, the socially and educationally backward class or such other group having disadvantage owing to social, cultural, economical, geographical, linguistic, gender or such other factor, as may be specified by the appropriate Government, by notification.

The implementation of the right to education is one of the means of preventing juvenile delinquency as well as promoting reintegration of children in conflict with the law. According to the CRC, one of the principles that should be observed in cases of deprivation of liberty of children is:

Every child of compulsory school age has the right to education suited to his/her needs and abilities, and designed to prepare him/her for return to society; in addition, every child should, when appropriate, receive vocational training in occupations likely to prepare him/her for future employment.

The JJB should pass orders for re-admission or continuation of the child in school if the child has been barred or suspended because of the pending inquiry or for havinglived in a CCI for any length of time. For instance, if a child in conflict with the law is dismissed from school for having spent six month in an Observation Home or Special Home, the advocate representing the child should urge the JJB to direct the school to re-admit him. The child should not be stigmatized and denied education because of his detention in a child care institution or the allegations against him.

Additionally, with a view to ensure the child's reintegration, the advocate should request the JJB or the Children's Court dealing with the matter as a JJB would, to pass additional orders under Section 18(2), JJ Act, 2015, requiring the child to attend school or attend a vocational training centre.

14. Right to child friendly procedures and ambience

The JJ Act, 2015 and JJ Model Rules, 2016 mandate the police, JJB, and the Children's Court to follow child friendly procedures while dealing with a child.

Article 14.2, Beijing Rules states, The proceedings shall be conducive to the best interests of the juvenile and shall be conducted in an atmosphere of understanding, which shall allow the juvenile to participate therein and to express herself or himself freely.

The JJ Act, 2015 and the JJ Model Rules, 2016, specify procedures that should be followed by the police apprehending a child alleged to be in conflict with the law, some of which are as follows: The child should not be sent to a police lock-up or kept in a jail, and should be transferred to the Child Welfare Police Officer (CWPO) at the earliest. If the child is denied bail by the police, the child should be sent to an Observation Home till the time of production before the Board, which should be done within 24 hours of apprehension.

The child should not be handcuffed, chained or otherwise fettered and no force or coercion should be used against the child. The child should be interviewed at the SJPU or child friendly premises or at a child friendly corner in a police station. The atmosphere should not such that the child does not feel it is a police station or that the child is under custodial interrogation. An advocate representing a child alleged to be in conflict with the law should verify whether these procedures were adhered to by the police. The breach should be brought to the attention of the JJB, but it should also be ensured that the child and the child's family are protected against reprisals. In case of regular use of force against children alleged to be in conflict with the law, a complaint could be addressed to the National Human Rights Commission or State Human Rights Commission.

A submission could also be made to the High Court Committee on Juvenile Justice as well. A writ petition could be filed before the High Court if the police torture results in loss of life or limbs.

Child-friendly procedures to be followed by the JJB According to the JJ Act, 2015, the venue should not be intimidating and should not resemble regular courts. The sitting arrangement should facilitate face- to-face interaction with the child. The JJB should not sit on a raised platform and there should be no barriers like witness box or bars between the JJB and the child. The JJB should also ensure that the proceedings are conducted in a simple manner and a child-friendly atmosphere is maintained during the proceedings. In their communication as well, the JJB should deploy child-friendly techniques and attitudes in respect of their body language, facial expression, eye contact, intonation and volume of voice while interacting with the child.

While recording the child's statement, the JJB should speak I a child-friendly manner to put the child at ease and enable the child to state the facts and circumstances fearlessly about the offence alleged, home and social surroundings and the influences that the child may have been subjected to.

Child-friendly procedures to be followed by the Children's Court

The JJ Model Rules, 2016, prescribes the procedures to be followed when the child is not tried as an adult, and when the child is tried as an adult. The proceedings should be held in camera if it decides not to try the child as anadult. The Children's Court should address the child in a child-friendly manner to put the child at ease and encourage the child to fearlessly state the facts and circumstances of the offence as well as the home, social surroundings and influences on the child when the child is not tried as anadult. The proceedings should not be conducted in an adversarial manner while examining witnesses and the powers under Section 165.

15. Evidence Act should be exercised

If the Children's Court decides to try the child as an adult, it should maintain a child friendly atmosphere and ensure that the final order includes an Individual Care Plan for the child. Neither the JJB nor the Children's Court can try a child jointly with a person who is not a child, even if they are co-accused in the same case. Further, if during inquiry, a person alleged to be CICL is found to be an adult after age determination, he cannot be tried along with a child. Based on this provision, achild transferred to the Children's Court by the JJB cannot betried with other adults.

16. Right to be heard

Article 12, UNCRC is one of the four general principles

of the UNCRC and states:

1. States Parties shall assure to the child who is capable of forming his or her own views the right to express those views freely in all matters affecting the child, the views of the child being given due weight in accordance with the age and maturity of the child.

2. For this purpose, the child shall in particular be provided the opportunity to be heard in any judicial and administrative proceeding affecting the child, either directly, or through a representative or anappropriate body, in a manner consistent with the procedural rules of national law.

Article 40(2)(b)(iv), UNCRC encompasses the right "to examine or have examined adverse witnesses and to obtain the participation and examination of witnesses on his or her behalf under conditions of equality". Article 40(2)(b)(vi), UNCRC requires the child to be provided free assistance of an interpreter if the child cannot or understand or speak the language.

The Committee on the Rights of the Child emphasizes the obvious relation between the right to be heard and the right to a fair trial. It also clarifies that a child should be able to communicate directly if it is in the child's best interest to do so. The right to participate is applicable at all stages and not just during the adjudication process. The Committee also underlined the significance of considering the child's views at every stage as well as when arriving at the final disposition: Alleging that the child is criminally responsible implies that he/she should be competent and able to effectively participate in the decisions regarding the most appropriate response to allegations of his/her infringement of the penal law. It goes without saying that the judges involved are responsible for taking the decisions. But to treat the child as a passive object does not recognize his/her rights nor does it contribute to an effective response to his/her behaviour. This also applies to the implementation of the measure(s) imposed. Research shows that an active engagement of the child in this implementation will, in most cases, contribute to a positive result.

Section 3(iii), JJ Act, 2015, recognises the right of every child to be heard and participate in decisions and processes affecting her or his interest. The child's views should be considered having regard to the child's age and maturity. The right to be heard requires the JJB to ensure the informed participation of the child and the child's parent or guardian in every step of the process. This would entail explaining the procedures, processes and their implications on the child at every step to ensure that the child and the child's parent or guardian are able to participate and makedecisions during the legal process. The JJB has a mandatory obligation to ensure the child's right to be heard. Fulfillment of this right requires that qualified an experienced interpreters and translators are provided to the child to enable the child to understand and participate in the proceedings.

17. Right to Privacy

The UNCRC and the Beijing Rules protect the right to privacy of all children in conflict with the law. Article 40(2)(b)(vii), UNCRC recognizes the right of a child alleged to have infringed the penal law "[t]o have his or her privacy fully respected at all stages of the proceedings." The Commentary to Rule 8, Beijing Rules which provides for the protection of privacy of juveniles recognizes that: Young persons are particularly susceptible to stigmatization. Criminological research into labelling processes has provided evidence of the detrimental effects (of different kinds) resulting from the permanent identification of young persons as "delinquent" or "criminal". Rule 8 also stresses the importance of protecting the juvenile from the adverse effects that may result from the publication in the mass media of information about the case (for example the names of young offenders, alleged or convicted). The interest of the individual should be protected and upheld, at least in principle.

The identity of a child in conflict with the law must be protected and the child's name, address, school or any identifying information cannot be published in any newspaper, magazine, news-sheet or audio-visual medial or other form of communication without prior written permission from the JJB. Such disclosure is permissible only if it is in the best interest of the child.

18. Protection from torture and ill-treatment

Article 37(a), UNCRC prohibits a child from being subjected to torture or other cruel, inhuman or degrading treatment or punishment. Under the JJ Act, 2015, theJJB should ensure that the child has not been subjected to any ill-treatment by thepolice or by any other person, including a lawyer or Probation Officer. Section 75(1), JJ Act, 2015 prescribes punishment for cruelty to child. It states: Whoever, having the actual charge of, or control over, a child, assaults, abandons, abuses, exposes or wilfully neglects the child or causes or procuresthe child to be assaulted, abandoned, abused, exposed or neglected in a manner likely to cause such child unnecessary mental or physical suffering, shall be punishable with imprisonment for a term which may extend to three years or with fine of one lakh rupees or with both.

The JJB can order the registration of a FIR if any offence has been committed against a child. This would include cruelty by the police or any person having the actual charge of, or control over a child. The JJ Act, 2015 prohibits corporal punishment with the aim of disciplining within child care institutions by persons-in-charge or employed in the institution. The breach of this provision will attract criminal proceedings and if found guilty, a person will be liable to a fine of Rs 10,000 on first conviction. Subsequent offences will make the person liable for imprisonment which may extend to three months or fine or both. A person convicted of corporal punishment will also be liable for dismissal from service and will be disbarred from working directly with children thereafter. If the management of the institution does not cooperate with orders of the CWC or JJB or court or State Government, then the person-in-charge of the management will be liable for punishment with imprisonment for a minimum term of three years imprisonment.

19. Right to be Protected from Sexual Offences

Article 19(1), UNCRC requires States Parties to: take all appropriate legislative, administrative, social and educational measures to protect the child from all forms of physical or mental violence,injury or abuse, neglect or negligent treatment, maltreatment or exploitation,including sexual abuse, while in the care of parent(s), legal guardian(s) or any other person who has the care of the child.

Rule 87(d), Havana Rules requires personnel of detention facilities for children in conflict with the law to "ensure the full protection of the physical and mental health of juveniles, including protection from physical, sexual and emotional abuse and exploitation," and to "take immediate action to secure medical attention whenever required".

The POCSO Act, 2012, criminalizes penetrative sexual assault, aggravated penetrative sexual assault, sexual assault, aggravated sexual assault, sexual harassment against a child and using a child for pornographic purposes. The term 'child' is defined to mean a person below 18 years. Penetrative sexual assault or sexual assault by a person on the management or staff of a Child Care Institution would constitute aggravated penetrative sexual assault or aggravated sexual assault. The POCSO Act places a mandatory duty to report a sexual offence against a child, upon any person who has apprehension that an offence is likely to be committed or has the knowledge that the offence has been committed. Failure to report the commission of an offence is a punishable offence and the penalty is higher, if the failure is on the part of a person-in-charge of any institution.

The JJ Model Rules, 2016, require CCI's to develop a system to ensure that no abuse, neglect and maltreatment takes place within the CCI. This would entail sensitizing the staff on recognizing abuse, neglect, and maltreatment and responding to them.

20. Right to rehabilitative dispositions

The JJ Act, 2015, provides for a range of rehabilitative dispositions under Section18(1) and (2). While disposing the matter, the JJB and the Children's Court shouldensure that the final order includes an ICP for the child's rehabilitation. A child found to be in conflict with the law by the Children's Court after a trial as an adult is entitled to "reformative services including educational services, skill development, alternative therapy such as counselling, behaviour modification therapy, and psychiatric support shall be provided to the child during the period of his stay in the place of safety." An advocate should ensure that the orders of the JJB and Children's Court are rehabilitative in nature.

21. Institutionalisation as a measure of last resort

According to the Beijing Rules, detention pending trial shall only be used as a measure of last resort and whenever possible, it should be replaced by alternative measures, like close supervision, intensive care or placement with a family or in an educational setting or home. Such detention should also be for the least period of time possible. While in detention pending trial, the juvenile should be kept separate from adults. In case of institutionalisation, priority should be given to 'open' over 'closed' institutions. Further, juveniles should be provided with care, protection and all necessary individual assistance (whether social, educational, vocational, psychological, medical or physical) that may be required in view of their age, sex and personality. Parents or guardians of the juvenile should have a right. According to the Beijing Rules, detention pending trial shall only be used as a measure of last resort and whenever possible, it should be replaced by alternative measures, like close supervision, intensive care or placement with a family or in an educational setting or home. Such detention should also be for the least period of time possible.

While in detention pending trial, the juvenile should be kept separate from adults. In case of institutionalisation, priority should be given to 'open' over 'closed' institutions. Further, juveniles should be provided with care, protection and all necessary individual assistance (whether social, educational, vocational, psychological, medical or physical) that may be required in view of their age, sex and personality.

22. Prohibition against imposition of death penalty or life imprisonment without the possibility of release

The JJB or the Children's Court cannot impose death penalty or life imprisonment without the possibility of release for any offence i.e., parole. Article 6(5), ICCPR prohibits the imposition of death penalty on persons who were below 18 years at the time of commission of the crime. Article 37(a), UNCRC prohibits capital punishment as well as life imprisonment without possibility of release for offences committed by persons below 18 years.

11

Objective of The Juvenile Justice Act

(a) to lay down a uniform legal framework for juvenile justice in the country so as to ensure that no child under any circumstance is lodged in jail or police lock-up. This is being ensured by establishing juvenile welfare Boards and Juvenile Court as primary processing agencies for neglected and delinquent juveniles;

(b) to provide for a specialised approach towards the prevention and treatment of juvenile delinquency in its full range in any situation of social mal-adjustment;

(c) to spell out the machinery and infrastructure required for the care, protection, treatment, development and rehabilitation of various categories of children coming within the perview of the juvenile justice system. This is proposed to be achieved by establishing observation homes, juvenile homes for neglected juveniles and special homes for delinquent juveniles;

(d) to establish norms and standards for the administration of juvenile justice in terms of investigation and prosecution, adjudication and disposition, and care, treatment and rehabilitation.

(e) to develop appropriate linkage and co-ordination between the formal system of juvenile justice and voluntary agencies engaged in the welfare of neglected or socially mal-adjusted children and to specifically define the areas of their responsibilities and roles;

(f) to constitute special offences in relation to juveniles and provide for punishment therefore; and, (g) to bring the operation of the juvenile justice system in the country in conformity with United Nations Standard Minimum Rules for the Administration of Juvenile Justice.

Thus at the normative level a sincere effort has been made to standardize and reinforce the juvenile justice system according to international standards. The Act aims at replacing the traditional mechanism for dealing with children in conflict with law as had been developed under the Children's Act in various States and Union Territories. The Act propounds a new concept of juvenile justice within the overall framework of social justice as enshrined in the Constitution of India. It symbolises a response to the changing socio cultural and economic conditions that affect juveniles, in terms of an equal sharing of opportunities for their growth and fulfilment.

Besides a thorough restructuring of the juvenile correctional system, the Act contemplates a vigorous use of the inherent potentials of the community for dealing with erring juveniles within the mainstream of social life. The scheme for the rehabilitation of the socially maladjusted juveniles is based on an individualized care, re-education and vocational training as essential means of their reintegration into the society. The new approach undoubtedly places an onerous responsibility on the State to mobilise all possible resources of the family,the community and social organizations in tackling the problem of juvenile social mal-adjustment in its full range.

Salient Features of the Act

The progressive features of the Juvenile Justice Act,1986, as compared to the provisions of the existing Children Acts of most of the states(not all states) are quite significant. Before we go ahead with a brief discussion of the main features it is worth mentioning that the present Juvenile Justice Act,1986 is more or less a reproduction of Children Act,1960 as amended in 1978. Similar situation is there in relation to the Children Acts of some other States, like Andhra Pradesh Children Act,1977, The Bombay Children Act,1948, Haryana Children Act,1974. In comparison to Children Act,1960 which is applicable to all the Union Territories, though it had not been enforced in all the Union Territories like Chandigarh, Lakshadweep till replacement by the Juvenile Justice Act,1986, only marginal changes can be noticed. Besides this the nomenclature under Children Act,1960 of words - "Child" and "Children Homes" has also been changed to "Juvenile" and "Juvenile Homes" respectively under the Juvenile Justice Act, 1986.

The broad features of the legal framework of the Juvenile Justice Act, 1986 can be classified in the following order:

a. The Act provides for a differential approach in the processing of the neglected juveniles vis-a-vis the delinquent. While neglected children would be produced before the Juvenile Welfare Board, the delinquents sire to be dealt with by the Juvenile Court. No person will be appointed as a member of the Board or a magistrate in the Juvenile Court unless he or she has special knowledge of child psychology and child welfare. The Juvenile Welfare Board and the Juvenile Court have been empowered for the transferability of cases brought before them on the basis of the necessary screening. Among the various circumstances to be taken into consideration in making an order under the Act, the state of physical and mental health of the juvenile and his welfare interest have to be ascertained as an additional requirement

b. The definition of ''neglected juveniles" has been construed more precisely. This is to ensure that only those juveniles who are likely to be abused, exploited, and inducted into criminogenic life and are in need of legal support to be weaned away from such situations Eire processed through law. The earlier definitions of 'neglected child', 'destitute child', 'uncontrollable child', etc., under different Children Acts were so vague to render the poor to be deprived of his basic right to freedom. A juvenile will now be separated from his parent or guardian only if the latter is unfit or incapacitated to exercise proper control. At the same time, legal protection has been extended to all juvenile being abused or exploited for immoral or illegal purposes or unconscionable gain. Of course, a juvenile who is found begging or who lives in a brothel or with a prostitute or frequently goes to any place used for the purpose of prostitution or is found to associate with any prostitute or any other person who leads an immoral, drunken, or depraved life is duly covered within the scope of 'neglected child'.

c. The procedure of handling neglected or delinquent juveniles at various stages of apprehension, processing and placement have been rationalised from the viewpoint of the protection of their basic rights as are not inconsistent with the requirements of m the law. A neglected child may be brought before the competent authority not only by a police officer but also by any other person or organization authorised for the purpose. This provision should enable social workers Find voluntary welfare organisations to increasingly assume the responsibility of referral of neglected juveniles to appropriate care. Apart from prohibiting the confinement of juveniles in a police lock-up or jail, his contact with the police has been considerably reduced. During the pendencyof the case before the competent authority, a provision has been made for the placement of the juvenile with any person or voluntary institution as considered fit. It is now specifically provided that an enquiry regarding a juvenile under this Act shall be held expeditiously and shall ordinarily be completed within a period of three months from the date of its commencement, unless, for special reasons to be recorded in writing, the competent authority otherwise directs.

d. The Act lays down a wide range of dispositional alternatives open to the competent authority, with preference to family/community based placement. The neglected juvenile will be sent to a juvenile home only if his care with a parent, guardian, or fit person or fit institution is not found conducive. For juvenile delinquent also, institutional care will be resorted to only as the last measure, in cases where restoration to parent, release on advice/ admonition, placement on probation, care under fit person/fit institution or discharge or fine is not considered appropriate. In both the cases, the care of the juvenile with his own family or substitute, family or within the community is considered more congenial for normal growth and development of the juvenile. Even when the juvenile is sent to a juvenile home or a special home, there is a definite provision for his conditional discharge or transfer or transfer to a fit person or a fit institution. This approach would provide for a considerable amount of flexibility in the treatment of the juvenile in keeping with his behavioural development and responsiveness to therapeutic devices.

e. Observation homes are contemplated for the temporary reception of juveniles during the pendency of an enquiry, when their placement with parents, guardians, or places of safety has not been feasible. Any institution other than an observation home established or maintained by the government may be recognised as an observation home. Every observation home is required under the Act not only to provide for the juvenile facilities for accommodation, maintenance, medical examination and treatment but also for useful occupation. There is a mandatory provision regarding the framing of rules for the management of observation homes, including the nature and standards of 76 services to be maintained therein

f. For neglected juveniles in need of institutional treatment, juvenile homes are required to be established or maintained by the government or voluntary institutions to be certified as such. Such juvenile homes will not only provide for the juvenile the facilities for accommodation, maintenance, education, vocational training and rehabilitation but would also ensure the development of his character and abilities as well as necessary training for protecting himself against moral danger or exploitation. The nature and standards of services are to be spelt out in rules. The focus on education, vocational training and rehabilitation is an important feature of institutional living.

g. Similarly, for delinquent juveniles, special homes are required to be set up or voluntary institutions certified as such. Social homes have to offer suitable facilities for accommodation, maintenance, education, vocational training and rehabilitation as well as for the development of their character and ability and reformative training, so as to ensure an all rounded growth and development of their individual personality. An important provision of the Act relates to the classification and separation of delinquent juveniles on the basis of age and nature of offences committed by them.

h. The Act contains a comprehensive provision regarding the establishment or recognition of after-care organisations for taking care of juveniles discharged from juvenile homes or special homes or special homes and for the purpose of enabling them to lead an honest, industrious and useful life. Specific rules are to be formulated for the relevant scheme as also for the nature and standards of organisations. The mandate calls for a systematic approach towards bridging the gap between the institutional treatment and the process of assimilation into the society.

i. Offences in respect of juveniles have been redefined in keeping with the newly-emerging problems faced by them. For instance, employment of juveniles for begging is liable to be punished by imprisonment for a term which may extend to three years along been with fine. Similar penal sanctions have/provided for giving intoxicating liquor or narcotic drugs as psychotropic substances to juveniles or for the exploitation of juvenile employees. More significantly, a new provision has been made to the effect that where an act or omission constitutes an offence punishable under this Act and also under any other Central or State Act,then I notwithstanding anything contained in any law for the time being in force, the offender found guilty of such offence shall be liable to punishment only under such Act as provides for punishment which is greater in degree.

j. Consequent upon the enactment of the Narcotic Drugs and Psychotropic Substances Act,1985 providing inter alia, for the establishment and notification of treatment centres for drug addicts, a provision has been made for the transfer of juveniles addicted to drugs to such treatment centres as in the case of juveniles of 90 unsound mind and those suffering for leprosy.

k. A new provision has been incorporated for the creation of a fund to be exclusively utilised for the welfare and rehabilitation of juveniles dealt with under this Act. Such a fund may be raised from voluntary donations, contributions or subscriptions made by 91 individuals or organizations. This surely opens a definite avenue of generating public support and participation in building up an effective system of juvenile justice.

l. The Act requires the State Government to constitute advisory boards to advise on matters relating to the establishment and maintenance of homes, mobilisation of resources, provision of facilities for education, training and rehabilitation of neglected and delinquent juveniles and co-ordination among various official.

An overview of the Act, especially in the context of facilities that have been desired under the Act and what has been actually created so for, gives an impression that the reformative and rehabilitation apparatus barely exists in fact. It appears as if legislation has been pushing ahead of reality. Legislation, of course, has a tendency to do so. If all the facilities which were prescribed by the Children Act,1960 for the use of juvenile justice system had come into existence in sufficiency the old system would not perhaps have been found wanting. As it is we have a new system which besides having introducing uniformity at all India level, has certain positive merits which, with patience, understanding and hard work, can be made to work in time, and to its optimum level, as the facilities materialise. In fact, the system as envisaged by the Juvenile Justice Act,1986 can serve as an ideal, a goal to be persued with relentless efforts in the years to come. Let us hope and wish that it does not take too long for the sake of our children in need of care, protection, reformation and rehabilitation.

Thus, the Juvenile Justice Act,1986 represents a very ambitious blueprint of a system to be established under the Act. In keeping with the International norms for the administration of juvenile justice, the Act calls for a thorough reorganisation of the existing system. There is a clear stress upon the involvement of voluntary sector and community based treatment for a better operation of the whole system. New infrastructure and mobilization of human and material resources in a better and co-ordinated manner has to be planned in order to make the system under the Act work at its desired level. Though in the 7th Five Year Plan a provision for providing better treatment to socially maladjusted children has been made but it has not yet produced desired results due to lack of proper co-ordination between the various departments of the States and also Central and State Social Welfare departments.

It is hoped that the past experience of two years will be a good pointer for better management and for optimum operation of the juvenile justice system as a whole. Punjab State is among the first few States to opt for the new system and the first necessary step towards the new goal has already been taken by enforcing the Juvenile Justice Act with effect from 2nd of Oct 1987 along with the adoption of necessary Rules under the new Act. Much more has to be done. Still it is a welcome move towards a better future for our juveniles in dis tress. A beginning has to be there in order to reach at the end and that begirding has taken place.

12

Philosophical Principle Behind Juvenile Homes

The State parties are obligated to recognize the right and treat an accused child in a manner which promotes and facilitates child's sense of dignity, and reinforce child's respect for fundamental freedom and human rights (Convention on the Rights of the Child, Article 40 (1)). The rationale behind differential treatment recognizes the child's inability to cope with unfavorable environment, to comprehend the consequences of his conduct which results in disproportionate reaction (Report of the Indian Jails Committee, 1919-20). Adolescence is a developing transitionary temporary phase resulting in heightened risk taking and decreased self regulation which adult prisons fail to address (Court on Its Own Motion v. Dept. of Women and Child, 2012). A child is considered a national asset, and incarceration in a jail may lead to dwarfing the development of a child, coarsening his conscienceand exposure to baneful influences (Sheela Barse v Union of India, 1986). The obligation to establish conformity of the legal procedure with desirability of promoting rehabilitation of the juvenile and the mandate to separate juvenile offenders from adult criminals is ensured through rehabilitation of juveniles in observation homes (UN General Assembly, International Covenant on Civil and Political Rights, 16 December 1966).

Therefore, the primary objective behind observation homes is to protect minors from incarceration and detention, and to keep them separated from the psyche of adult offenders. Reformation and rehabilitation, and not punishment are the guiding principle for mechanism regarding juvenile delinquents. Along with safety, protection and care of the alleged child in conflict with the law, it must also be ensured that complete legal aid is available, by ensuring attendance to every hearing and explaining to the child of the process involved (Ministry of Women and Child Development, 2017).

Observation homes are also run on the notion of Individual Care Plans considering each child's familial situation, mental and physical status quo through counseling sessions, conducting aptitude test for vocational training and consultations with physical, mental and education professionals. The Delhi High Court Juvenile Justice Committee further impressed upon the Department of Women and Child Development to introduce more vocational trainings, to be imparted for the juveniles, so that when they leave the institutions, they become capable to earn money for their livelihood and reintegrate themselves in the society.

The Juvenile Justice Act acknowledges every right of a child, irrespective of the gravity of the crime committed. Being a non-custodial legislation, the Act ensures toprovide an umbrella protection to the right of a delinquent to institutionalized treatment, right to bail within 24 hours, right to free legal consultation, right to re-unite with family and right to protection of identity. It also safeguards negative rights such as right against corporal punishment, right against FIR(excluding heinous offences) and right against handcuff, lock-up and disqualification from the society. In order to safeguard these rights, the Central Government, the State Governments and other agencies are guided by the following principles (The Juvenile Justice (Care and Protection) Act, 2015, S. 3) based on which observation homes function.

Principle of presumption of innocence

Any child shall be presumed to be an innocent of any mala fide or criminal intent up tothe age of eighteen years. This principle presumes that anything done by the child or the child in conflict with law has been done without mens rea or malafide intention. This principle operates right from the initiation of the proceedings and ends at the aftercare programme. It simply states that whatever be the act committed and whatever be thecircumstances and whether it is done by himself or under the control of the adults or withthe influence of peer group should always be considered that the said Act has been committed without mens era i.e. the Principle of presumption of innocence should beapplied for all those activities which has been covered or explicitly stated in the Rule.

Principle of dignity and worth

All human beings shall be treated with equal dignity and rights. This principle mandates the agencies involved in the JJ Act are to treat the child with dignity and worth and not to label, stigmatize or discriminate the child. It also mandates the authorities to respect the personal identity and such other things relating to the child right from initial apprehension till the aftercare is over.

Principle of participation

Every child shall have a right to be heard and to

participate in all processes and decisions affecting his interest and the child's views shall be taken into consideration with due regard to the age and maturity of the child. Children's right to be heard shall include creation of developmentally appropriate tools and processes of interacting with the child, promoting children's active involvement in decisions regarding their own lives and providing opportunities for discussion and debate.

Right to be heard in administrative and judicial proceedings is also one of the fundamental principles of juvenile jurisprudence, including the Convention on the Rights of the Child, the Beijing Rules, and the General Comment No.10 of the UNCRC Committee. Article 12 (2) of CRC requires that a child be provided with the opportunity to be heard in any judicial oradministrative proceedings affecting the child, either directly or through a representative or an appropriate body in a manner consistent with the procedural rules of national law.

Principle of best interest

All decisions regarding the child shall be based on the primary consideration that they are in the best interest of the child and to help the child to develop full potential. Children differ from adults in their physical and psychological development and their emotional and educational needs. Such differences constitute the basis for the lesser culpability ofchildren in conflict with the law. These and other differences are the reasons for a separate juvenile justice system and require a different treatment for children. The protection of the best interests of the child means, for instance, that the traditional objectives of criminal justice, such as repression/ retribution, must give way to rehabilitation and restorative justice objectives in dealing with child offenders.

A further explanation of this principle can be found in

Article 3 of the Convention on the Rights of the Child says that

a) Primary consideration to the child's best interests 'in all actions concerning children, whether undertaken by public or private social welfare institutions, courts of law, administrative authorities or legislative bodies'.

b) Taking appropriate legislative and administrative measures to ensure well-being of children by providing necessary protection and care. c) Ensuring compliance of institutions, services and facilities responsible for the care or protection of children with the standards established by competent authorities, particularly in the areas of safety, health, in the number and suitability of their staff, as well as competent supervision.

Principle of family responsibility

In a family, a child is introduced to emotions like love and security. The social values and cultural aspects of the community are inculcated in the child within the family background i.e. the primary responsibility of care, nurture and protection of the child shall be that of the biological family or adoptive or foster parents, as the case may be.

Though many functions of family like education, health, recreation etc. are being taken up by other social institutions, the family retains its importance as a constituent entity and building block of all societies and communities. Thus, the principle of family responsibility plays a vital role in the administration of juvenile justice as an informal care and all authorities functioning under the JJA should take all the necessary decisions of the child with the active involvement of the family of the children, who are in conflict with law.

Principle of safety

All measures shall be taken to ensure that the child is safe and is not subjected to any harm, abuse or maltreatment while in contact with the care and protection system, and thereafter. It also mandates that the state shall not use restrictive measures in the name of safety of the child.

Positive measures

All resources are to be mobilized including those of family and community, forpromoting the well-being, facilitating development of identity and providing an inclusive and enabling environment, to reduce vulnerabilities of children and the need for intervention under this Act. The term positive measures include the avenues for health, education, relationships, livelihoods, leisure, creativity and play . The Principle wants to achieve the objective of facilitation in establishing the personal identity of the child and to enable the child to equip himself to achieve the developments in all the processes relating to the individual growth.

Principle of non-stigmatizing semantics

Adversarial or accusatory words are not to be used in the processes pertaining to a child. For example, it mandates to avoid the following wordings in the process of administration of Justice relating to children, who are in conflict with law. It includes the following arrest, remand, accused, charge sheet, trial, prosecution, warrant, summons, conviction, inmate, delinquent, neglected, custody or jail.

Principle of non-waiver of rights

No waiver of any of the right of the child is permissible or valid, whether sought by the child or person acting on behalf of the child, or a Board or a Committee and any non-exercise of a fundamental right shall not amount to waiver.

Article 2 of the Convention on the Rights of the Child insists on "appropriate measures to ensure that the child is protected against all forms of discrimination or punishment on the basis of the status, activities, expressed opinions, or beliefs of the child's parents, legal guardians, or family members". In its General Comment Number 10: Children's Rights in Juvenile Justice, (United Nations, Geneva), the UN Committee on the Rights of the Child stated the need for taking "necessary action to ensure that children are treated equally with particular attention to 'de facto discrimination and disparities' that affect vulnerable groups of children such as 'children who are indigenous, children with disabilities and children who are repeatedly in contact with the law (recidivists)".

The Beijing Rules too emphasize that all children must be treated equally and that the Standard Minimum Rules listed therein should be "applied to juvenile offenders impartially, without distinction of any kind, for example as to race, colour, sex,language, religion, political or other opinions, national or social origin, property, birth or other status." (Rule 2 (1)).

Principle of equality and non-discrimination

There shall be no discrimination against a child on any grounds including sex, caste, ethnicity, place of birth, disability, health, status, race, religion, cultural practices, work, activity or behaviour of the child in conflict with law or that of his parents or guardians, or the civil and political status of the child. This principle also includes that equality of access, opportunity and treatment shall be provided to every child.

Principle of right to privacy and confidentiality

Every child shall have a right to protection of his privacy and confidentiality, by all means and throughout the judicial process. In other words, no report in any newspaper, magazine, news-sheet or audio-visual media or other forms of communication regarding any inquiry or investigation or judicial procedure, shall disclose the name, address or school or any other particular, which may lead to the identification of a child in conflict with law or a child in need of care and protection or a child victim or witness of a crime.

No staff/stakeholder should divulge/ disclose any details to anyone regarding any case of CNCP (Child in Need of Care and Protection) or CCL (Children in Conflict with Law) or identification of the same.

Principle of institutionalization as a measure of last resort

Deprivation of liberty has negative consequences for the child's harmonious development and seriously hampers his/her reintegration in society. Deprivation of liberty, including arrest, detention and imprisonment, should be used only as a measure of last resort and for the shortest appropriate period of time, so that the child's right to development is fully respected and ensured. A child shall be placed in institutional care as a step of last resort after making a reasonable inquiry. The principle objective of institutionalization and detention in the juvenile justice system should be to ensure that the offender is free of criminal behaviour as soon as possible.

Principle of repatriation and restoration

Every child in the juvenile justice system shall have the right to be re-united with his family at the earliest and to be restored to the same socio-economic and cultural status that he was in, before coming under the purview of this Act, unless such restoration and repatriation is not in his best interest. (This principle should be read alongside of principle of family responsibility).

Principle of fresh start

While children who have offended must be held

accountable for their action, every child has the capacity to change for the better and must have a second chance - a right to a fresh start. The principle of fresh start signifies a new beginning in the life of the child in conflict with law. All past records of any child under the Juvenile Justice system should be erased except in special circumstances.

Principle of diversion

Measures for dealing with children in conflict with law without resorting to judicial proceedings shall be promoted unless it is in the best interest of the child or the society as a whole.

Principles of natural justice

Basic procedural standards of fairness shall be adhered to, including the right to a fair hearing, rule against bias and the right to review, by all persons or bodies, acting in a judicial capacity under this Act.

13

Management of Juvenile Homes

The Act stipulates the obligation to constitute Juvenile Justice Boards in every district to deal with juvenile cases in conflict with law (The Juvenile Justice (Care and Protection of Children) Act, 2015, S. 4), as well as Child Welfare Committees to deal with cases of children who need care and protection (The Juvenile Justice (Care and Protection of Children) Act, 2015, S. 29). The Juvenile Justice Board shall complete each inquiry within a period of four months after the first summary inquiry and only in exceptional cases (trans-national criminality, large number of accused, and inordinate delay of witnesses) shall extend to two more months on, with prior recording of reasons by the Board ((The Juvenile Justice (Care and Protection of Children) Act, 2015, S. 13).

A Management Committee is also mandated to monitor, every month, the progress of every juvenile and to review the minimum standard of care, housing, infrastructure, medical facilities and services like food, water, hygiene, education, and vocational training, and grievance reddressal, provisions of legal aid services, release or restoration.

Functioning

As soon as a child in conflict with law is apprehended by the police, he shall be produced before the juvenile justice board within twenty four hours(The Juvenile Justice (Care and Protection of Children) Act, 2015, S. 4), by the special juvenile police or designated police officer under whose charge such juvenile was placed(The Juvenile Justice (Care and Protection of Children) Act, 2015, S. 10(1)). According to the JJ Rules (2016), in case of failure to produce the alleged child before the Board owing to odd hours or distance, the child shall be kept in an observation home by the Child Welfare Police Officer and shall be produced before the board within twenty four hours of apprehending.

Section 12 makes it absolutely clear that the child alleged to be in conflict of law should be released on bail, and if such release apprehends exposure to physical, moral or psychological dangers, then the child should be kept in observation homes and safety place, but not jails. Conventionally, the apprehended children aredetained for temporary reception, care and rehabilitation up to four months in these observation homes, under probation and, after due enquiry and satisfaction of the allegation, the child shall be transferred to a fit facility. Transfer of the child out of the district or State shall be considered in case of apprehension of danger, to ensure protection and safety of the child.

Infrastructure and services

According to Rule 21 ((The Juvenile Justice (Care and Protection of Children) Model Rules, 2016) and Section 41 (The Juvenile Justice (Care and Protection of Children) Act, 2015), at the time of registration, the State Government shall determine and record capacity & purpose of the institution; and shall register the institution as a Children's Home/ Open Shelter/ Specialized Adoption Agency/ Observation Home/

Special Home (Place of Safety), as the case may be.

As per Rule 40 (3) of JJ Rules (2016),

> *"A child care institution should have the building or accommodation with dormitories, classrooms, sickroom/first aid room, counseling and guidance room, workshop, playground, kitchen, dining hall, store room, recreation room, library, office room, residence for Superintendent and adequate toilets/bathrooms as per the prescribed norms in the said rule."*

For each institution with a capacity of fifty children, two dormitories (1000 sp. ft. each), two classrooms (300 sq. ft. each), a distinct sickroom, kitchen, dining hall, office rooms, workshop and residence of superintendent shall be present. Whereas, eight separate toilets and separate bathrooms (25 sp. ft. each) and a sufficient area shall be designated as playground, covering a total of 8495 sq. ft area for each home (The Juvenile Justice (Care and Protection of Children) Model Rules, 2016, R. 22). All boundaries walls shall constitute standard height to prevent intruders, or children from eloping.

Integrated Child Protection Scheme (ICPS) guidelines (Kapil, U.,2002) further mandate conformity of the functioning of child care institutions with the minimum standards of accommodation laid under the rules. Fundamental requisites such as food, shelter, clothing and medical attention, and special equipments like hearing aid, Braille kit, wheel chairs and other suitable prosthetic aids must not be compromised with. Education along with referral services like skill development and recreational activities, de-addiction and vocational training must be incorporated (Right of Children to Free and Compulsory Education Act, 2009). For efficiency, Individual Child Care Plan for each child shall be formulated in accordance with familial situation, peer and neighborhood influences, determine interest through counseling, interaction with family, training and counseling,

Location

The observation home should be centrally located, with easy access to medical and transport resources, police station, parks, schools vocational training and residential area to keep them connected with the community and avert the apprehension of isolation and seclusion. The functioning and infrastructure of observation homes, under no circumstances, shall resemble a prison.

Receiving children in protective custody

At the time of admission in the observation home, the juvenile shall be received at the reception area while the formalities are conducted. Once the admission of the child in the observation home is complete, the child shall be placed in the reception dormitory for the first fourteen days, and then admitted into the observation home(The Juvenile Justice (Care and Protection of Children) Model Rules, 2016, R. 69(D) and F(2)). The reception area shall be equipped with graphic display material, and shall conduct an orientation session to elucidate the role of the observation home, expected conduct, and redressal mechanisms. This facilitates the child to get accustomed and comfortable with the terms of institutional care. The reception room shall embody dormitory with toilet and bathing area, and adequate table and seating area for storage of register and files. A separate premise shall be designated as a visiting area for the purpose of providing privacy to the parents or guardian who may visit(The Juvenile Justice (Care and Protection of Children) Model Rules, 2016, R. 74).

The child should be provided a comfortable atmosphere, to give him time to settle down. A gentle search and seizure ensuring children are frisked, patted down and searched in a manner that does not hinder their dignity, while girl child must be searched by female staff member only. Any personal belongings or valuables of each child shall be disinfected, recorded and kept under safe keeping until they are returned to child when he leaves. Admission of a child shall be supervised by the Child Welfare Police Officer or any authorized person through a written requisition. A medical checkup and segregation in quarantine rooms in case of contagious disease, on the recommendation of the doctor, shall be ascertained.

Segregation

The foremost necessity is to create separate premises for children in conflict with law and children in need of care and protection, in order to prevent baleful influence of the former over the latter. Segregation of boys and girls is imperative while it is advisable to group children on the basis of age, nature of offence, care required, health, and length of stay order(The Juvenile Justice (Care and Protection of Children) Model Rules, 2016, R. 29(1) and 55(2)). It isalso stipulated to segregate accommodation for boys and girls upto 12 years, 13 – 15 years and 16 years and above(The Juvenile Justice (Care and Protection of Children) Model Rules, 2016, R. 16(2)).

Education, Training and Recreational activities

Considering the accommodation of each child in observation home is short term and temporary, the children's education(The Juvenile Justice (Care and Protection of Children) Model Rules, 2016, R. 36) and training (The Juvenile Justice (Care and Protection of Children) Model Rules, 2016, R. 32) shall continue uninterrupted. The children, who were enrolled in a school, must be immediately admitted to the same class. If the child is not in a formal system or has never been in one before, their education shall be assessed through aptitude test and interview. It is advisable to provide distinct and diverse options for vocational training to enable them to pick a lucrative option (The Juvenile Justice (Care and Protection of Children) Model Rules, 2016, R. 37) which shall help them become financially independent in the long run. An aptitude test to determine vocation training is rational, and they shall be encouraged to prefer vocation training for a trade they could easily continue during their stay and even when they return home.

Another pertinent aspect of training is Life Skill Education which shall focus on adaptive and positive behavior facilitating rehabilitation (The Juvenile Justice (Care and Protection of Children) Model Rules, 2016, R. 65). The Life Skill Education module for observation home shall be confined to four months, ranging from life skills to skill based modules for 10-12 sessions, and therapeutic specific module for the latter sessions. These may embrace literacy, worth ethic, managing expenses, decision making, negotiation and public speaking. While, therapeutic specific modules may include anger management sessions, risk taking behavior, dealing with extreme emotions or addictions. Active recreational activities such as singing, dancing, gardening and passive recreational activities such as watching movies, listening to music shall be encouraged during weekends or public holidays (The Juvenile Justice (Care and Protection of Children) Model Rules, 2016, R. 38). De-addiction programmes followed by progress reports also play a significant role in rehabilitation.

Sponsoring summer and winter camps to unplug monotonous routine and including Art resource persons, and sports meets shall enable mental and physical development. The superintendent of the observation homes shall develop networking to partner with Institute of Technical Instruction, National Skill Development Corporation, vocational counselors, NGOs and placement agencies for introduction of children to sports, recreational activities, internships, career counseling, and industry human resource requirements.

Paramedical and Psychologist

Observation homes shall contain a paramedical and psychologist team, for a routine medical examination. A doctor and ambulance services shall be ensured on a 24x7 basis for emergencies. A baseline investigation to determine blood count, urine routine, HIV, Hepatitis, allergy or addictions is indispensable(The Juvenile Justice (Care and Protection of Children) Model Rules, 2016, R. 26). While, a cognitive session with counselor for mental history to determine need for services of therapist or psychiatric social worker shall be prolific. Females shall be checked for deficiencies, if any, followed by a nutrition plan and medicine prescription as required.

Participation through Committees

Forming Committees plays a major role in engaging children systematically in issues so as to gain their insight, criticism and elicit their assistance in running the observation home. Suggestive tenure of these committees is two months, where children nominate themselves for election to not more than two committees (Ministry of women and child development, 2017). These may include food, hygiene and behavioral conduct committees where the elicit help with menu, hygiene of the premises, decisions in cases of bad conduct such as fight, conflicts or disagreements. Other recreational committees such as literacy, sports committee, cultural committee for organizing cultural events, suggesting sports and games through consensus and assistance for library. The committee shall also be responsible for placing complaints before the Superintendent in cases of discrepancies.

Protection norms and emergency

Presence of distinct male and female guards, duty roster and security personnel are indispensable(The Juvenile Justice (Care and Protection of Children) Model Rules, 2016, R. 67). The home door shall remain locked and entry into the homes shall be after a verified standard process including identity verification and scrutinizing personal belongings. A regular check of electronics, monitoring content on television, safe custody of harmful substances, and surprise search and seizure for prohibited substance shall be conducted. Regular patrolling by the local police and surprise visits by person-in-charge not less than once in a week is necessary to ensure efficiency(The Juvenile Justice (Care and Protection of Children) Model Rules, 2016, R. 67(7)).

An exhaustive proceeding in case of emergency such as eloping or missing children, death by suicide or natural cause, disaster and epidemics has been formulated. A report with the police station and to the board or children's court, and immediate search for nearby places such as railway station bus stand should be conducted by the staff. The police shall collect a recent photograph and fill the missing personal information form with copies to missing person squad, Legal services Authority (of eloped and bordering districts both), State and National Crime Bureau (The Juvenile Justice (Care and Protection of Children) Model Rules, 2016, R. 92). A strict action against the staff in case of security lapse is necessary but no punitive action against the child who eloped is advisable. However, in case of recurrent eloping, the child should be produced before the children's court.

In case of death by suicide an immediate autopsy and in case of natural cause a medical examination report to determine the cause of death is mandatory(The Juvenile Justice (Care and Protection of Children) Model Rules, 2016, R. 75). In case a child dies within 24 hours, it should be reported to the police, district medical officer and the parents/ guardians without delay or prejudice. A formal entry should be registered with the photograph of the child in concerned registers and hospital records, whereas photography and videography of the incident of suicide should be kept for future evidence. The body of the child should be handed to the parents for last rites, whereas in cases where no contact with parents, the person-in-charge should do it, in accordance with the hospital rules(The Juvenile Justice (Care and Protection of Children) Model Rules, 2016, R. 65). Quarantining children with infectious diseases, arrangement of medical treatment in epidemic outbreaks, disinfection the roomsare essential steps for prevention. There should be an efficient disaster management strategy, delegating each staff role and function in case of such disasters for evacuation, and a frequent mock drill should be held each month(The Juvenile Justice (Care and Protection of Children) Model Rules, 2016, R. 67).

Code of Conduct: staff, visitors and children

Corporal punishment, threatening, mocking or foul language of any kind is prohibited, which may affect the child mentally or physically. Never shall they sleep alone with any child, initiate physical contact or develop sexual relations. They are not entitled to issue any personal work to the children or use their position for own benefit of any kind. Every institution shall ensure a system that ascertains no abuse, neglect and maltreatment, and staff should be trained for how to respond to these abuses(The Juvenile Justice (Care and Protection of Children) Model Rules, 2016, R. 76).

In case a staff perpetrates abuse, exploitation the matter shall be reported to the probation officer and children court, and an immediate prevention of any contact with children during the period of inquiry. UNCRC (1991, A. 37(a)) protects and JJ Act (2015, S. 75) punishes a police or person who has charge over the child including lawyer and probation officer assaults, abandons, abuses exposes or willfully neglects or subjects the child to any cruel or inhuman torture. Cases of sexual abuse should be mandatorily reported to the SJPU(The Juvenile Justice (Care and Protection of Children) Model Rules, 2016, R. 76) under the Protection of Children from Sexual Offences Act (2012).

Every child should be trained to follow standards of good behavior such as respective everyone, never threatening, abusing, discriminating or ragging a child. Assault or sexual abuse is prohibited and potential child abuse or mistreatment cases shall be reported. The Person-in-control may manage the infringement accordingly, giving due thought to the opinion of the Child Care Committee, and the dignity of the child. The action being taken against such child should be in consideration of the age, nature and degree of violation. The purpose of punishment should be to embark a sense of understanding about what they did wrong(The Juvenile Justice (Care and Protection of Children) Act, 2015, S. 82) and may range from formal warning, assigning housekeeping tasks, writing he won'trepeat the mistake hundred time, or forfeiture of privilege to watch television or go for a recreational activity. Rewards and benefits in case of exceptional good behavior should be provided, which shall further inspire other children.

However, in case of abuse, exploitation or any other crime committed, the person in charge should immediately file a report before the board and the special juvenile police unit, followed by an order of investigation((The Juvenile Justice (Care and Protection of Children) Act, 2015, S. 30). Immediate inquiry, legal aid and counseling for the victim and transfer of the child to another institution. Assistance shall also be elicited from voluntary organizations, child rights experts, mental health experts or crisis intervention centres in dealing with matters of abuse and exploitation of children in aninstitution(The Juvenile Justice (Care and Protection of Children) Model Rules, 2016, R. 76).

Complaint and redressal mechanism

Rule 39 (The Juvenile Justice (Care and Protection of Children) Model Rules, 2016) stipulates setting up of a redressal mechanism and a children suggestion box at a place closer and easily accessible from the child care institution. This should remain with the chairperson of the management committee and the suggestion should be reviewed regularly, while the child remains anonymous. The quorum should include five members, including two members of Children's Committees, Chairperson of the Management Committee, Member of the Board and the Person-in-charge of the Child Care Institution for conducting emergency meeting. In case of serious allegation against a staff or person-in-charge he should not be included in such meetings, where issues and the actions that could be sought are discussed. The child should be given access to CHILDLINE through hotline facility, where the child can speak in privacy.

Repatriation or transfer

If the enquiry determines that the child hails from a place outside the jurisdiction of the board(The Juvenile Justice (Care and Protection of Children) Model Rules, 2016, R. 81), or resides in a place or city which is closer to another observation home, the transfer shall be ordered immediatelyafter due consultation with the board. If the child hails from another state, a repatriation order by the board to the special juvenile police unit should finalise the transfer wand within 15 days of the order, the child should be escorted accompanied by SJPU or DCPU with prior medical examination of the child (The Juvenile Justice (Care and Protection of Children) Model Rules, 2016, R. 81(2)). Whereas, in the case if the child hails from another country, the State Government should be immediately informed. The State Government shall bear the expenses for immediate transfer in consultation with the Ministry of External Affairs (The Juvenile Justice (Care and Protection of Children) Model Rules, 2016, R. 81).

In cases where the child is found to have committed the offence he shall be immediately transferred to a special home. If the child completes 18 years without completing the time period for rehabilitation and reformation as per the order of the board, he shall be transferred from special home to place of safety. Whereas, from place of safety to prison as the last resort, in case a child aged 16-18 years found guilty of committing a heinous offence, but no reformation is witnessed in the assessment conducted at the end of his stay in the place of safety.

The child may be released on bail, acquitted if found innocent, released after admonition or transferred to a special home if found guilty (The Juvenile Justice (Care and Protection of Children) Act, 2015, S. 19).Each release should be informed to the ICP, which shall form the decision. The release of child on bail, the PO/CWO should counsel the parents and the child continue education and vocational training during the period of trial, update them about the date and time of hearings and ensure they attend each hearing. In case of requirement of after care or supervision as determine by the ICP, the PO should undertake necessary follow up visits to place of residence, place of employment, school asking the child to report to the PO(The Juvenile Justice (Care and Protection of Children) Act, 2015, S. 97). In case of release after admonition, the board should issue necessary direction the DCPU for arranging counseling, community service follow up, and supervision to ensure no repetition of offence(The Juvenile Justice (Care and Protection of Children) Act, 2015, S. 18).

Prior coordination with the parents should be ensured, informing them the reason and implications of the transfer or release, services offered in the new institution and frequent updates regarding the time and date of transfer. In case, the parents are unable to reach CCI on the day of release owing to financial constraint, their expenses should be borne by the person in charge or make arrangements to send the child to the parent house with a CWO from SJPU. The valuable and other belongings which were kept in the custody of home during the stay should be returned. In case a girl child has no place to go after release, or the day of release falls on a public holiday, the officer in charge should allow them to stay until further arrangement subject to the approval of the Children's Court (The Juvenile Justice (Care and Protection of Children) Model Rules, 2016, R. 79).

14

Special Home For Juvenile Delinquents

The Juvenile Justice Act, 1986 provides that the State Government may establish and maintain as many Special Homes as may be necessary for the reception of delinquent juveniles under the Act. Every such home shall not only provide the juvenile with accommodation, maintenance and facilities for education, vocational training and rehabilitation, but also provide him with facilities for the development of his character and abilities and give him necessary training for his reformation and shall also perform such other functions as may be prescribed to ensure all round growth and developmment of his personality. The State Government has in the Rules framed under the Juvenile Justice Act, 1986 provided for the standards and nature of services to be maintained by the Special Homes. Besides this the Rules provide for the classification of delinquents on the basis of age and nature of offence committed by them.

Objective of care in Special Home:

The objective of care in a special home is to:

1. Provide reformative services including education, skill

development, counselling, behaviour modification therapy, and psychiatric support during the period of stay in the Special Home.

2. Formulate and/or review and/or implement an Individual Care Plan for each child based on understanding the child's background (familial situation, peer and neighborhood influences, positive influences), needs and interests, through the use of appropriate methods including counselling sessions, interaction with the child's family, home visits, aptitude testing for education and vocational training, and consultation with physical and mental health professionals.
3. Ensure that children accept responsibility and take accountability for the crime they were found to have committed, and begin a process of healing and transformation.
4. Preparing the child for reintegration into the family and community with skills and a plan to ensure that he/she will not commit crime again.

Approach to provision of services in a Special Home:

Since SH is a reformative care facility which houses children found to have committed offences for a period up to 3 years, and is not a prison, the approach to provision of services the institution as a whole, and its duty bearers must be one which ensures that:

1. Children are not treated as criminals or prisoners and shall be provided with as much liberty as is possible.
2. Upon entering the institution, children must be reassured that the SH and its staff are there to support them throughout the period of stay.
3. Children are counselled through a process of taking accountability and responsibility for their actions.
4. Children must be supported to make a fresh start with

their lives, and must be supported to become emotionally and financially self-reliant as they reintegrate back into society.

Deprivation of liberty throughout the period of stay in a Special Home will not achieve reformation of children effectively, unless it is accompanied by a process where children begin to take accountability for their actions, and find ways in which they can help to repair the harm they have caused. Taking accountability helps offenders to come to terms with what they have done, accept it, find ways to repair the harm they have caused {even if, sometimes their actions have been very grave}, and accept themselves. It helps them find purpose, move forward with their lives and avoid crime in the future. Creating a positive environment and facilitating this process from the time the child enters the Special Home during the reception and orientation stage.

Receiving a Child in the Special Home

The Receiving Officer shall conduct all procedure related to receiving the child. Receive and welcome the child into the Special Home in a gentle manner.Undertake introductions of self and child and explain to the child what receiving/ admitting him/her will entail giving the child some time to settle down, explain the procedure of receiving the child to him/her: The steps involved and how long will it take.Under take search and seizure in accordance with provisions in the Act and Rules, however, ensuring that children are frisked and searched in a manner which is gentle, decent, and does not violate their dignity. Girl child must be searched by a female staff member only. No foul language (swear words or threats) shall be used and no rough handling of children shall take place.

Verify the identity of the child and the order of the Board or the Children's Court:

1. Record all personal information of the child in an admission register
2. The date of admission and the date that the child is to be discharged shall also berecorded in the Admission and Discharge Register.
3. Check and record identity marks on the child
4. Make a record of personal belongings, cash, other valuables of every childreceived by the home, in the personal belongings and other relevant registers,
5. If the child is being transferred from an OH, take a hand-over of the case file ofthe child.
6. The case file should contain all assessments- psycho-social, educational andvocational; reports of the counselling and conferencing sessions conducted by the counsellor and PO; progress report; medical records and the Individual CarePlan.
7. Take personal belongings, cash, other valuables of the children safe keeping until thesame is returned to the child at the time that he/she is discharged from the Special Home.
8. Explain the order of the JJB and the sentence to the child and explain to him what theobjective of stay is in the Special Home, and what would be expected of him/her, andwhat should be expected from the home.
9. The child shall be examined by the medical officer, who shall record the state ofhealth of the child, and of any wound or mark on his body and any observation whichthe medical officer thinks fit, a copy of which shall be placed in the medical record ofthe child.
10. The child shall be provided with medical care if it is required, and may be placedin the segregation unit, or admitted in hospital if necessary.

Every SH should have established linkages with

outside specialists and community-based welfare agencies, psychologist, psychiatrist, child guidance clinic, hospital and local doctors, open school, Jan Shikshan Sansthan etc. A Directory of Services should be accessible to every SH.Children who have been transferred from the OH and have undergone the above process in the OH would not have to undertake the educational and vocational training assessment. However, if the child wants to change his/her vocation, stream of education, the process may be repeated to find the most appropriate option for the child.

Vocational Training

A child may be placed in a SH for a period for up to 3 years, which is adequate time for him/her to learn a skill or vocation, which would provide him/her livelihood upon being reintegrated back into society.Every child should be encouraged to take up vocations which he/she may be able to continue training either after returning home to his/her family or during the period of stay in the Special Home.

The counsellor should administer an aptitude test to help the child to decide his preference of vocational course if it has not been administered before in case the child has not been admitted from the OH. If the child was in the OH and had opted for a particular vocational training course, and now would like to change to something else, he/she shall be given the opportunity to do so.

The counsellor should arrange meetings/exposure between CCI and workshop in-charge and other technicians for the child to understand better clarity about the different vocational courses being offered. This residential care facility provides reformation and rehabilitation services to children found to have committed crime for a period of up to three years. Vocational training should be one of the most important components of the program. The objectives of vocational training shall be as under:

1. To introduce a curriculum that gives children theoretical, technical and practicalknowledge of the vocations which are offered.
2. To give children formal vocational training which should offer examinations andcertification upon completion of the course.
3. Impart skills and knowledge that make children financially self-reliant when theyleave the CCI.
4. To ensure that children get the opportunity to find the most appropriate trade, andare not forced to make a choice from restricted options available in the CCI.
5. To ensure that facilities are made available to children to go to ITI and othertechnical institutes for training.

Education

If the child is not in a formal system of schooling at the time of admission in the Special Home or has never been in one before, the education level shall be assessed by teacher on the basis of tests and interview with the child. Every child irrespective of age must be encouraged to take up formal education and efforts at the special home must be towards keeping the child in the system, and bringing those who are not to a level where they can be integrated with the formal system of education.

Physical Health

Every child should undergo a medical examination within 24 hours of their admission into the special home or immediately if there is a health emergency/health need.If the child is suffering from a contagious disease at the time of the admission into the special home, he/she should be kept in the quarantine room on prescription by the doctor.

Mental Health

The counsellor should have a session with every child

newly admitted in the SH.If the counsellor suspects that the child is showing any symptoms suggestive of a mental health condition, services of psychiatrist/psychologist/psychiatric social worker should be sought after discussion with the PO/Case Worker/CWO and with approval of the Superintendent.

Individual Case Conference

Every child shall have a daily interaction with the PO/caseworker assigned charge of his/her care. There shall also be an individual interaction with the PO/case worker under the supervision of the PO, to ensure that the child's progress is monitored, on a weekly basis.Records of each case conference session shall be maintained and placed in the case file of the child.

Free legal aid

Every child is entitled to understand the legal process he/she has to go through, the stages of the case, what to expect at each production and that he/she has right to receive free legal aid from the State.Free legal aid shall be rendered by the CCI via legal aid institutions of the State Legal Services Authority, District Legal Service Authority, or from the DCPU. The Superintendent would ascertain from the child [and/or his/her guardian] if they have legal assistance and if they have legal aid from the DLSA/SLSA etc. In case they need, the Superintendent would take all steps to ensure that the legal aid lawyer from DLSA/SLSA is provided to the child. The Board/Children's Court may also deploy the services of the student legal services volunteers and nongovernmental organisation volunteers in para-legal tasks such as contacting the parents of the child and gathering relevant social and rehabilitative information about him/her

Safety and Security

The Superintendent is in-charge to ensure the safety

and security of all children residingin the CCI. The infrastructure requirements for safety and security have been discussedand may be referred to in the section on 3Infrastructure of CCI'. Following measures forthe safety and security of the children shall have to be taken.

The excessive use of discipline and security measures and of a punishing approach canalso be the origin of violence and anger, of reinforced psychological disorder, traumaand depression that can lead to violent behavior, self-harm or suicide. This needs to bekept in mind while dealing with any kind of disciplinary issues in the CCI.

Visits and interactions with the children

Communication and contact with family and significant people should form an essential part of a child's rehabilitation and preparation for re-integration in the society. Parents know more about their children than anyone else, and thus, are often the key source of invaluable and essential information. All efforts should be made topromote improved relationship between the child and his/her family wherever dysfunctional, unless it is not in the best interests of the child. Parents and families can provide key support when the child is released from CCI.

As per Rule 74 of the JJ Model Rules 2016, every child in the Child Care Institution may be permitted to have one meeting in a week with his relatives.The minimum time of the meeting shall not be less than 30 minutes. In special cases, where parents or guardians have travelled a long distance from another State or District, the Person-in-charge may allow the parents or guardians entry into the premises and a meeting with their children on other days on confirmation of their identity and they being reported not to have been involved in subjecting the child to abuse and exploitation.There should be a day and time designated for the weekly meeting and the parents should be informed of the same at the time the child is being admitted into the CCI. A newly received child shall be permitted to meet his parent or guardian or family member on their first visit on any day.If the parents are not present at the time of the admission, the CWO/PO/Case worker shall establish contact with them and inform them about the weekly meeting and encourage them to meet the child every week.

If there are problems between child and his family, the CWO/PO/Caseworker shall facilitate the interactions between child and his family, sit in on meetings until necessary. No meeting shall be permitted with the parent or guardian or relatives where such visitors have been found to be involved in subjecting the child to violence, abuse and exploitation or carrying any prohibited articles, except with the express permission granted by the Board or the Committee or the Children's Court or when such meeting has been specifically directed by the counsellor of the child.Every child shall be allowed to write two letters in a week to his parent or guardian or to his relatives. Necessary stationary and postage for the letters shall be provided by the Person-in-charge.

The Person-in-charge may peruse any letter written by or to the child and may for reasons to be noted in the case file of the child, refuse to deliver or issue the letter. A report of the same shall be prepared and placed before the Management Committee. A copy of the report shall be retained on the case file and another copy shall be sent to the Board or the Children's Court or the Committee. Every child shall be allowed to bring any written communication for the purpose of handing over to the Board or the Committee or the Children's Court, as the case may be, and be provided stationary, etc. for the same.The Person-in-charge may allow a child to speak with his parents or guardians on telephone once a week under supervision of the Child Welfare Officer or Case Worker or Probation Officer and record shall be duly maintained of such calls.

Transfer, Release and After Care

Pre-release planning

The PO/CWO/Case Worker shall begin the pre-release planning three months prior to the date of release of the child from the Special Home. During the pre-release planning, the PO/CWO/Case Worker shall ensure family therapy sessions with the child and his family. The sessions should aim at setting expectations of the child from the family members and vice-versa. Individual therapy sessions by the counsellor/psychiatric social worker: The child to be helped to identify adults who can provide the needed emotional and social support to the child, what his future aspirations are and what actions on the part of the child are required to make a progress towards achieving his/her future aspirations, exploring options for education, training, apprenticeship/job etc., Updating the ICP: The ICP of the child needs to be updated prior to the release and have to be approved by the Board/Children's Court. Each part of the ICP shall be updated with the child and the respective staff responsible for it. Parents shall also be consulted during the process of updating of the ICP.

The ICP shall be approved by the management committee and the Superintendent shall sign on the ICP before it is presented before the JJB. The ICP should be sent to JJB/Children's Court for approval 2 months prior to the release of the child. Linkages with the DCPU and other non-governmental organizations: On approval of the ICP by the JJB, the PO/CWO/Case Worker shall approach the DCPU and other NGOs in the area where the child is going to reside to help the child in the process of social reintegration, and to ensure that the ICP is being implemented.

Transfer

Transfer of a child from one CCI to another CCI or a fit facility can be made in the following circumstances and as ordered by the Board/Children's Court:

During the inquiry, if it is found that the child hails from a place outside the jurisdiction of the Board shall if satisfied after due inquiry that it is in the best interest of the child and after due consulation with the Board of the child's home district, order the transfer of the child as soon as possible, to the said Board, along with such order and relevant documents and send a copy of the order stating the reasons for and circumstances of such transfer to the State Government and District Child Protection Unit. Observation Home to a Special Home on completion of inquiry and if the child is found to have committed the offence.

Special Home to a Place of Safety if the child completes 18 years and has not completed the time period for rehabilitation and reformation as per the orders of the Board Place of Safety to prison, in case a child aged 16-18 years is found to have committed a heinous crime and is found to not have been reformed in the assessment conducted at the end of his stay(completion of 21 years of age) in a place of safety.

Release

As per JJ Act, 2015, when a child is kept in a Special home, on a report of a probation officer or social worker or of Government or a voluntary or non-governmental organisation, the Board may consider, the release of such child, either absolutely oron such conditions as it may think fit to impose, permitting the child to live with parents or guardian or under the supervision of any authorized person named in the order, willing to receive and take charge, educate and train the child, for some useful trade or calling or to look after the child for rehabilitation.

If child has been released on a temporary basis, the time during which the child is notpresent in the concerned home in pursuance of the permission granted shall be deemed to be part of the time for which the child is liable to be kept in the children or special home.

In case of a child in conflict with law who fails to fulfil the conditions set by the Board, the time for which he is still liable to be kept in the institution shall be extended by the Board for a period equivalent to the time which lapses due to such failure. The Person-in-charge of the Child Care Institution shall maintain a roster of the cases of children to be released on the expiry of the period of stay as ordered by the Board or the Children's Court.

After care

The State Government shall prepare a programme for children who have to leave Child Care Institutions on attaining eighteen years of age by providing for their education, giving them employable skills and placement as well as providing them places for stay to facilitate their re-integration into the mainstream of society.

Any child who leaves a Child Care Institution may be provided after care till the age of twenty-one years on the order of the Board or the Children's Court, and in exceptional circumstances ,for two more years on completing twenty-one years of age as per Rule 25(2) of JJ Model Rules 2016. The District Child Protection Unit shall prepare and maintain a list of organisations, institutions and individuals interested in providing after care as per their area of interest such as education, medical support, nutrition, vocational training etc. and the same shall be forwarded to the Board and all Child Care Institutions for their record.

The CCI shall, through counselling support and other

programmes, prepare the young adults for life outside the Institution and for the After Care programme. The process of transition from institutional care to after care should take into consideration the gender, maturity and particular circumstances of the child. Young adults leaving institutional care should be encouraged to take part in the planning of their own after care.

An aptitude test /career guidance should be done by the counselor of DCPU with the help of a technically qualified person/agency before placing the young adult into appropriate after care programmes. If the Person-in-Charge, PO and other home staff involved in the process of rehabilitation of the child, during the pre-release planning are of the opinion that thechild needs further supervision, care and support before their reintegration into the community, the child shall be referred to after care organization.

The Probation Officer or the Child Welfare Officer or Case Worker or social worker, shall prepare a post release plan and submit the same to the Board or the Committee, two months before the child is due to leave the Child Care Institution, recommending after care for such child, as per the needs of the child.

In case the child does not have parents, guardians or relatives, the child shall be referred to the CWC as part of the pre-release planning who then refer the child to an institution for children in care and protection. The referral to CWC shall also be made if the Person-in-Charge, PO and team are of the opinion that going to the family and the locality is not in the best interest of the child or If the child does not desire to his/her to return to his family or if suitable inquiry it is established that the family is not the conducive place in the best interest of the child, the child may be placed in a group home or a hostel, the funds for which shall b provided under provisions for after care in ICPS.

Children who are placed in after care programme, shall be provided funds by the State Government for their essential expenses; such funds shall be transferred directly to their bank accounts. The Person-in-charge on direction of Board or Children's court shall provide the child with such tools, as may be necessary; to start a work or business subject to such maximum cost as may be fixed by the institution/State Govt. which shall also form part of the post-release plan.

After Care Services

The Board or the Children's Court, while monitoring the post release plan will also examine the effectiveness of the aftercare programme, particularly whether it is being utilized for the purpose for which it has been granted and the progress made by the child as a result of such after-care programme. If the Superintendent and the PO, during the pre-release find that the child needs after care post their release from the home, they shall update the same in the ICP and present a plan for the same to the JJB.

The decision for after care and the plan for after care shall be done in consultation with the child, his/her parents/ guardian and the staff involved in the rehabilitative process. The objective of after-care shall be to enable children to adapt to the society and during their stay in aftercare homes children are encouraged to move away from an institution-based life to a community.

The services of the After-care programme are: Community group housing on a temporary basis for groups of 6-8 persons. Provision of stipend during the course of vocational training or scholarships for higher education and support till the person gets employment. Arrangements for skill training and placement in commercial establishments through coordination with National Skill Development Programme, Indian Institute for Skill Training and other such Central/ State Government programmes and corporates etc.

Provision of a counsellor to stay in regular contact with such persons to discuss their rehabilitation plans. Provision of creative outlets for channel listing their energy and to tide over the crisis periods in their lives. Arrangement of loans and subsidies for persons in after-care, aspiring to set up entrepreneurial activities and Encouragement to sustain themselves without State or institutional support. At the time of release, if there is a plan for after-care, the Board/Children's Courtshall designate a Probation Officer/ Case worker to supervise/monitor the child's progress in after-care.

15

Place of Safety

The Place of Safety is an institutional mechanism in the Juvenile Justice System which provides, as the name suggests, a safe place of stay for a particular category of children i.e. children in conflict with law, who have either committed a certain category of offence and are in a particular age group or regarding whom it is perceived that any other existing residential arrangement will not be suitable for them or in their best interest.

As per Section 2(46) of JJ Act,2015, "place of safety" means any place or institution, not being a police lockup or jail, established separately or attached to an observation home or a special home, as the case may be, the person in-charge of which is willing to receive and take care of the children alleged or found to be in conflict with law, by an order of the Board or the Children's Court, both during inquiry and ongoing rehabilitation after having been found guilty for a period and purpose as specified in the order.

Further, as per Rule 29 (1) (iii) of JJ Model Rules, 2016, following are the categories of Place of Safety:

(a) for children in the age group of 16 to18 years alleged to have committed heinous offence pending inquiry;

(b) for children in the age group of 16 to 18 years found to be involved in heinous offence upon completion of inquiry;

(c) for persons above 18 years alleged to have committed offence when they were below the age of 18 years pending inquiry;

(d) for persons above 18 years found to be involved in offence upon completion ofinquiry;

(e) for children as per the orders of the Board under clause (g) of sub-section (1) of section 18 of the Act. This institution was not created to house any child entering the juvenile justice system, but instead to address the specific and special needs of a special category of children. It is also understood thereby that children in conflict with law, especially those who are alleged or found to have committed heinous offences are children who are most vulnerable and need specialized, focused and designed interventions which would ensure the emotional, physical, social and economical well being of such children.

These interventions are to be based on a comprehensive assessment of the child and of the circumstances in which she /he has entered the JJ System. This is essential as research regarding developmental history of children and impact of adverse childhood experiences has demonstrated that failure to achieve developmental goals and childhood trauma result in health especially mental health and behavioural malfunctioning which often leads to offences of such grave nature. Assessment would therefore include understanding of the child's developmental history and the gaps therein and the socio economic background, as well as the circumstances in which the offence was committed. Unless such an assessment is carried out and by persons trained to do so, interventions administered would not be effective. Rehabilitation without assessment would neither prevent recidivism nor ensure that the child leads a meaningful life once she/he has left the institution.

Comprehensive assessment of the child, need based interventions and skilled caregivers are the three most critical components of any Place of Safety.

Provisions

The Place of Safety has been defined and detailed in Section 2, (46) and Section 49,of the JJ Act, 2015 and in Rule 29 (iii) of the JJ Model Rules, 2016. There are other provisions and rules which also provide information regarding this mechanism. These include inter alia, provisions and rules related to, infrastructure, registration, categories of children in conflict with law who are to be placed therein, rehabilitation services, standards of care etc.

Features

Place of Safety is:

i) A Child Care Institution (CCI) and all the provisions and norms related to CCIs under the Act and Rules framed there under will apply to this institution.

ii) ii) Child-friendly and in no way shall it look like a jail or lock-up.

iii) To be attached with an observation home or a special home or established separately.

iv) An institution where Children are placed by the order of Juvenile Justice Boardor the Children's Court for a period and purpose as detailed in the order.

v) To house both category of children i.e. who are alleged to have committed anoffence regarding which inquiry is ongoing or children who have been found guilty after completion of inquiry.

vi) A place wherein safe shelter and/or services for rehabilitation, is provided, as mandated. While the Place of Safety may be a segregated facility, it should provide all required services for the rehabilitation of the child in his or her best interest.

vii) For placement of children, alleged or found to have committed heinous offencesor children who have not been granted bail in their best interest, irrespective ofthe offence or those whose matters have been referred to the Children's Courtpost assessment by the Board.

viii) A safe space for children till they attain the age of twenty-one years and thereafter, the person shall be transferred, by orders of the Children's Court , toan adult correctional facility or Jail.

Purpose

The Place of safety established will further emphasise on:-

i) Promoting the well being of the child by formulating individual care plans based on comprehensive assessment for the rehabilitation of the child.

ii) An assessment of a child which must include the child's developmental history, school history as well as social history. This would specially apply to children who have committed a heinous offence Interaction with the family and other persons associated with the child should not be restricted to the period ofinquiry; instead it should be continued and a regular component of assessmentof the child carried out during long term care and rehabilitation. These could bescheduled at the same time as Board/Children's Court hearings.

iii) Providing services for each child, as per the comprehensive assessment done, which will include inter alia, educational services, skill development, counseling, behaviour modification therapy and psychiatric support etc. for rehabilitation of the child. This will be reviewed periodically by the Probation Officer or Legal cum Probation Officer appointed by the State Governmentunder DCPU) as directed by the Board/Children's Court.

iv) Positive measures should be taken to provide a safe and secure atmosphere and accident free infrastructure which helps the child over come trauma, identify thepersonality and behavioural patterns which are harmful to self and to learn selfregulation, build trusting relationships and re-establish faith in a better life. Theultimate aim being to reduce vulnerabilities and minimize the internal risks ofre-offending.

v) Ensuring that the child is safe and that child protection mechanism such assuggestion book, suggestion box, children's committee etc. are in place.

Infrastructure

The JJ Act, 2015 and Rules framed there under mandate that every State must have at least one Place of Safety set up by the State Government. Place of Safety as mentioned earlier may be attached to an Observation Home or Special Home or established separately. Place of Safety shall also be registered as per procedure laid down under section 41 of JJ Act, 2015 for registration of Child Care Institutions. At the time of registration, the State Government shall determine and record the capacity and purpose of the Place of Safety.

Norms related to infrastructure, under the Act and Rules there under, which are applicable to all CCIs, will also have to be adhered to in the Place of Safety. These include norms for type of rooms, size of rooms, number of rooms, lighting, safety and hygiene, space for outdoor activities etc.

Additionally, norms related to segregation of children based on gender and age differences also have to be maintained. Children who are placed in Place of Safety will include:

a) Children in the age group of 16 to 18 years alleged to have committed heinous offence pending inquiry;

b) Children in the age group of 16 to 18 years found to be involved in heinous offence upon completion of inquiry;

c) Persons above 18 years alleged to have committed offence when they were below the age of 18 years pending inquiry;

d) Persons above 18 years found to be involved in offence upon completion of inquiry;

e) Children as per the orders of the Board under clause (g) of sub-section (1) of section 18 of the JJ Act, 2015.

Standards of care

Just as for infrastructure and other provisions, standards of care for Place of Safety are also to be the same as those applicable for other Child Care Institutions. These include inter alia standards for clothing, bedding, toiletries, sanitation and hygiene, safety and security measures such as CCTV Cameras & Fire Extinguishers, Emergency Contact Numbers etc., documentation, nutrition, vocational training, education, medical care, protection from abuse (Childline 1098, Grievance and Complaint Mechanisms etc.), recreation etc.

Even if the Place of Safety is a separate facility not attached to an Observation or Special Home, it should therefore provide all required services for the rehabilitation of the child in the best interest of the child. The Place of Safety must also have in place, the committees mandated under the JJ Act, 2015 for monitoring the administration of the CCI and the progress of every child and for ensuring child participation i.e. the management and children's committees respectively.

Additionally a Child Protection Policy (CPP) must also be in place which is signed by all staff members, displayed in the CCI premises. This must include verification of all staff and monitoring of entry and exit of persons from CCI.

Staff

Staff requirement for the Place of Safety shall be based on the special needs of the children placed there and which shall be as provided under the JJ Act, 2015, JJ Model Rules, 2016 and the ICPS. The State Government may make provisions for additional staff if required. The credentials and background of all staff recruited for the Place of Safety must be verified.

Training

The importance of skills and knowledge in staff, who are to administer, monitor and execute a programme in a Place of Safety need special training and sensitization. The focus must be on building the knowledge, skills and the attitudes / mindset required to work in a setting of such a nature. Training of staff, induction orientation as well as on job training, to be based on a training need assessment and include short term and long term training plans.

Training content and methodology needs to be drawn up in consultation with experts from relevant fields such as Law, Training, Mental Health, Business Management, Entrepreneurship Development etc. Latest methodologies and knowledge related to Children in conflict with law, must be, contextualized and incorporated in training content.

16

The Concept of Restorative Justive

Children who break the law do not do so of their own free will, but rather as a result of restricted opportunities available for their development. Such opportunities become even more restricted once they enter the criminal justice system. Children from risk groups that could get in conflict with the law are often victims of abuse and neglect, negligent and poor parenting and economic difficulties. Juvenile delinquency is not a success story, but evidence of the society failing to ensure protective environment for its children. Labelling such children results in exclusion from society rather than assistance in their rehabilitation. If child offenders continue being criminalized while at the same time being denied a second chance that they deserve, their chances will lead to nothing but their reoffending when they grow up.

These children need support while they are still children. The efforts of the communities/societies to rehabilitate such children are insufficient for their developmental needs. There is need for capacity building of communities to increase their understanding of such issues and also to deal with children. The child's personality is developed throughout his or her development and depends on the stage of development: the child becomes capable of taking responsibility for its needs, acts, health and safety. Therefore, the society has the duty to ensure and provide special protection to children.

Need for Restorative Justice as a tool for Rehabilitation of CCL

Unlike retributive justice where the focus is on the crime and violation of law, restorative justice aims at resolving the problem through reconciliation and improvement of the newly created situation. The victim's needs are respected and the offender takes responsibility, which shows he understands the consequences of his crime.

Restorative justice is a new view of the criminal legal system which focuses more on the restoration of the damage that the crime has done to people and their mutual relations rather than the punishment of the offender. Restorative justice is a process that involves all who are directly or indirectly affected by the crime in an attempt to decide how best to restore the damage. There are three categories of those directly affected by the crime, namely victims, offenders and their immediate community, whose needs are to receive restitution for material and non-material damage, take responsibility and restore good relations in the community respectively. Therefore, the emphasis is on the needs of people, individuals, respect for their human values and their personalities, and not just the punishment of the offender.

Restorative justice is based on the following four basic principles:

i) establish balance disrupted by a crime or conflict in the community and society and restoring the damage made;

ii) make restitution to the victim;

iii) create conditions for the offender to understand and take responsibility for his acts;

iv) assist in changing and promoting future behaviour of the offender.

The victims feel that children are let off easily even when they commit a serious offence or repeat offences. Juvenile Justice adopted the path of reformation of children found to have committed an offence through various community based reformative and rehabilitative measures and using institutionalization as a measure of last resort and for the minimum period till suitable community based alternatives are found for them. For example, as per section 18 of JJ Act, 2015, the JJB can pass orders for CCL such as: direct the child to participate in group counselling and similar activities; order the child to perform community service under the supervision of an organisation or institution, or a specified person, persons or group of personsidentified by the Board.

In designing a community service programme for children above the age of 14 years, such as maintaining a park, serving the elderly, helping at a local hospital or nursing home, serving disabled children, serving as traffic volunteers. The JJB may combine the restorative justice approach by keeping in mind:

1. the nature of offence committed by the CCL
2. the circumstances of its commission
3. the impact on the victim
4. lessons that should be taught to the CCL
5. how the programme will help correcting the harm to the victim

Any offence is fit for restorative justice if it is applied

appropriately. Many countries in the world are using restorative justice to rehabilitate children who have committed crimes. The preconditions for adopting restorative practice in a given case are:

1. The CCL must accept commission of offence.
2. The CCL (and not their parents) must be ready to accept responsibility for correcting the wrong.
3. The CCL must be ready to apologies to the victim.
4. The victim will have a say in deciding what he/she want the CCL to do to make amends.
5. It cannot be demeaning the offender but must be focused on making good the harm caused.
6. The victim should be assisted in not demanding something which is beyond the means of the CCL to fulfill.

Restorative justice practices can also be used as a very effective positive disciplining tool amongst the children in CCIs as well. It is useful for conflict resolution amongst children and also when there is some peer harm involved. While this requires some training of the staff, it is not a complex process. It involves getting both parties (that have caused harm and that have been harmed) to agree to a conference where the victim can speak about the impact and the accused is also given a chance to explain his/her behaviour. It is a forum where people deal with wrong doing and conflict. The facilitator creates a safe space for everyone to participate. The facilitator does not influence the decisions taken by the participants but allows them all to speak and find their own solutions.

The labelling theory suggests that a person engages in deviant behaviour not only because of their own individual behaviour but also because of societal response. This means that when society labels an individual as deviant, they will eventually engage in that labelled deviant behaviour.

The reason for this is that society not only labels the person but it also sanctions and stigmatizes them. This reaction from society, including their peers, friends, and even family, effectively alienates them from society. They are perceived as a criminal and their previous behaviour is also redefined negatively to fit this perception.

This treatment changes the labelled person's self-perception and they begin to engage in deviant behaviour that conforms to the label that society has thrust upon them. They increasingly seek solace in subcultures. They interact with others who exhibit deviant behaviour, who accept this behaviour as 'normal'. This further pushes them into crime and deviance. They shield themselves from society, which is the only entity that can help them because it offers some normalcy. Thus, deviance becomes a lifestyle that is difficult to change. In essence, labelling "leads the deviant individual to follow a self-fulfilling prophecy of abidance to the ascribed label".

Under the Act, an individual between sixteen and eighteen years of age, who is accused of a heinous offence, is made to undergo extensive character and psychological evaluation. The JJB then decides whether they should be tried as an adult. When the JJB orders that a child be must tried as an adult, they effectively label the child a 'criminal'. The child gets the message that they do not deserve to be treated like other children – that they must be tried like an adult as they are beyond reform.

Further, trying a child like an adult exposes the child to a court situation where they are continuously exposed to a rigorous scrutiny of their actions, personality, and behaviour, and a formal judgement on their guilt is pronounced. To make matters worse, in certain districts, no Children's Courts have been designated. Consequently, children have to be tried like adults in the Court of a Sessions Judge. This is in direct contradiction to the more child-friendly environment that JJB proceedings seek to create.

The effect this has on an adolescent child is particularly strong because adolescence is the period in which children develop their social identity. An early experience in the criminal justice system can have long-term negative implications. They experience the conviction "not as a condemnation of their behaviour but as a condemnation of them". The pernicious impact of this labelling sticks with the child even after they are released from prison.

As per the Principle of Fresh Start, the records of juveniles are destroyed. This is done to provide the child with a fresh beginning and an opportunity to reintegrate into society without any stigma. However, the Act makes an exception for those who are tried as adults and mandates that their records must be maintained. Further, they do not have the right to not disclose their criminal antecedents. This would mean that they carry the label of a criminal for their entire life. This only serves to increase societal stigma and limits their educational and employment opportunities. It denies them a fresh start, serves as a constant reminder that they are 'criminals', and makes reintegration into society difficult for them. This labelling and subsequent stigmatisation alters their self-conception and as empirical research has found, increases recidivism.

References

1. Allison Morris and C. Brielle Maxwell, Restorative justice for Juveniles: Conferencing Mediation and Circcles, Oxford University Hart Publisging, 2001

2. Dwi Hapsari Retnaningrum and Manunggal K. Wardaya,

Perlindungan Terhadap Anak Yang Melakukan Tindak Pidana (Kajian Tentang Penyelesaian Secara Non-Litigasi Dalam Perkara Tindak Pidana Anak di Kabupaten Banyumas, Purbalingga, Banjarnegara, Kebumen, dan Cilacap), Research Report, FH UNSOED, 2011.

3. Elizabeth Hurlock, Development Psychology, A Life Span Approach, terjemahan Istiwidayanti & Sudjarwo, Psikologi Perkembangan, Jakarta: Penerbit Erlangga, 2000.

4. F. Pieter Hoefnagels. The Other Side Criminology, an Inversion on the Concept of Crime, Holland: Kluwer Deventer,1972

17

Realities of Juvenile Homes in India : Hell Holes

Accentuated in the national audit of NCPCR, dark and claustrophobic rooms with iron bars and locks on them, economic impetus for corruption, overcrowding, stale food and lack of functioning toilets 16 are just the tip of the iceberg. While a significant proportion of juveniles has been locked up in adult jails, those living in juveniles homes are in much worse condition. 67% of CICLs had reportedly been slapped, 30% were beaten severely, 32% had been whipped with a belt, 15% had been hung from the ceiling, and 1.7% had been sexually abused in the institutions which stand on the pillars of rehabilitation and corrective behaviour. While non-segregation on the basis of age, sex, mental health and nature of offence has always been overlooked, amalgamation of CICLs, CNCPs and mentally challenged juveniles together18 envision a despairing state of society. Forced subservience of CICLs for cleaning washrooms and corridors, and collecting money for the superiors, under the fear of being locked up in jails if resisted is dreadful. An unsettling image of these homes was unveiled when an 11 year old, a CNCP looking forward to return to his hometown, was found dead under mysterious circumstances.

Another horrific incident of a 10 year old female inmate found bleeding when transferred to Girl's Juvenile home, Hyderabad indicated brutal rape, serious state of shock and alleged absence of poor investigation by the police officials. Astonishingly, juveniles have also complained of sexual abuse by supervisors themselves, with details of torture, in a letter indicating abuse by the district probationary officer (DPO) when these juveniles tried to file a complaint. Ms Ganguly, advocating for the plight of juveniles says:

> "If you push young people into adulthood so early, they will behave like adults sans the cognitive ability to, and with whatever role models of adulthood around them."

Authorities estimate that as of June 2019, there are over four thousand inmates who could be children in prisons in Delhi. Putting children in adult prisons can often have adverse consequences. Prisons can serve as a school for criminals. Children can learn how to commit crimes and avoid detection from more experienced inmates. Further, they are exposed to an environment where prisoners commit crimes and acts of violence against each other. The children in prisons are forced to accept this violence as part of their daily life, and they soon adopt this anti-social subculture prevalent there.

They also face a greater risk of being physically or sexually abused in prisons. This abuse is perpetrated by other inmates and also by guards and prison officials, who are in a position of power. The brutalization of a child could destroy their sense of personhood and self-worth and make them resent the state and the system. This could aggravate their sense of not belonging in society and decrease their willingness to conform to societal norms.

Further, it is likely to give them the wrong idea about

the psychological benefits and acceptability of criminal behaviour. They harden themself as a self-defence mechanism and associate with gangs for the sake of protection. They may even brutalise other inmates. This could make children socially maladjusted and more violent and hostile.

Incarcerating children in adult prisons hampers their development. It particularly affects their identity formation. Prisons and jails, being retributive in nature, break down identities and do not help build new ones that represent societal norms. Juvenile homes, on the other hand, offer rehabilitative measures in a comparatively safer environment than prisons. Studies have found that juvenile homes prioritise rehabilitation – the children found the staff helpful and most of them felt confident that they would not reoffend. This was in complete contrast to those children who were incarcerated in adult prisons. Thus, juvenile homes, by virtue of their safer and rehabilitative environment, reduce the chances of recidivism as compared to prisons. As Dilulio wrote, "Jailing youth with adult felons under Spartan conditions will merely produce more street gladiators."

Sexual assault is the second type of treatment meted by the children in observation homes. In an incident, a 14-year-old juvenile from Jamnagar was sodomised allegedly by the four boys at the observation home on Gondal Road, Rajkot. They allegedly also beat four inmates with polymer pipes and two of the accused forced others to perform oral sex. They also filmed the victims naked. The peon who was on duty when the incident took place at the observation home, did not made any attempt to stop this incident or to report this incident. There are many surveys, and reported incidents of sexual abuse on children in observation homes. Many victims are threatened with knife and blades for sexual abuse.

This use of force also results in extensive injuries to

victims' genitalia, which facilitate transmission of sexually transmitted diseases (STDs). They are touched in disturbing ways, forced to expose genitalia and finally forced into sex. It has been found that in many cases the perpetrators are staff members including caretakers, security guards, etc in the observation homes. In most of the cases, the sexual assault continues for a longer period as victims are not ready to dissent and endure quietly in the absence of inspection. The incidents where, two minor girls were assaulted by the manager in Odisha observation home, or boys sodomised by guards and senior inmates at govt. home for boys, Delhi. Child rape is a common feature. A 2013 report by the Asian Centre for Human Rights (ACHR), states that juvenile justice homes have become India's hell holes where inmates are subjected to sexual assault and exploitation, torture and ill-treatment, apart from being forced to live in inhuman conditions. It highlights 39 cases of repeated sexual assault on children in juvenile justice homes, including government-run observation homes, children's homes, shelter homes and orphanages. Recently, the National Commission for Protection of Child Rights has reported that it has registered 77 complaints/cases concerning child abuse, sexual exploitation, torture, ill treatment, disappearance, running away of children, lack of residential facilities and otherirregularities committed in the child care institutions including observation and special homes across the country in four years.

Another situation which should be seriously considered is the nature and age of inmates in the observation home. Under the Act, juvenile alleged to have committed a bailable or non bailable offence are brought before the Juvenile Justice Board, where they are released under the supervision of a probation officer. Those juveniles, who are not released on bail by the Board, are sent to the observation home, pending inquiry. The juveniles who were alleged to have committed a serious offence were also housed in observation homes during the period of inquiry, which affect the mindset of junior inmates or those who were not party to serious offences.

It has been reported by the inmates that those juveniles who are alleged of committing offence for the second time or more, takes the position of senior inmates. Therefore in the observation homes there are two categories of inmates, junior and senior. Once junior inmates are tortured by the police authorities, they are then given to the senior inmates for further beatings and other abuses. As per one of the incident, in December 2013, the National Commission for Protection of Child Rights (NCPCR) received allegations of physical abuse in a juvenile observation home in Meerut, Uttar Pradesh. The allegations were made by a 17-year-old boy, who was among children who escaped from the home. He alleged that the mass escape was prompted by repeated instances of physical and sexual abuse of juveniles by older youths living in the observation home. Most of them were repeated offenders.

Observation homes take a little care of hygiene. As per the report of Careshare India, it was even called as 'pilla jail' because of the overburdening of inmates. In sharp contrast with the ambitiousgoals outlined by the Indian government in the Juvenile Justice Act, the life of children is more horrifying than the family environment they escaped and often more wretched than the life on the streets. According to one of the study, the food supplied by the government into these observation homes, i.e., three meals a day is considerably a meager portion which is hardly nutritious and largely inadequate. Many of them display obvious signs of malnutrition, when they are consumed out of hunger; they gave them painful stomach cramps.

"The dishes are not always washed after every meal. With the stale rice they are given for lunch and dinner, the children often find worms and cockroaches crawling over the leftovers from previous meals, still stuck to the plates."

The children's health conditions are a major cause of concern. Scarce hygiene, insufficient nutrition, and the lack of space render the children easy prey to a variety of highly contagious diseases. The children are allowed to change clothes very infrequently. The guards do not clean the halls and bathrooms, which are infested with cockroaches and lice. As a result many children develop skin infections, dysentery, herpes zoster, genital warts, and sexually transmitted diseases. The home also does not provide medicines or the manpower to take the children to the Government Hospital. Water shortage, lack of drainage systems, working toilets - all this makes the hygiene levels in the homes extremely low.

In India, under the current system, the child would have to serve their sentence until the age of twenty-one years in a remand home. Therefore, it may be argued that the effects of incarceration with adults are mitigated. However, as per the law, the child would be transferred to a jail after the age of twenty-one to serve the rest of their sentence.Thus, they would still be subject to the negative influence of prisons. This would nullify the effect of any rehabilitation that may have taken place in the juvenile home. On the other hand, after their time in a juvenile home, if the child were reintegrated into society with proper post-rehabilitative care, they would avoid the negative influences of prison altogether, thereby reducing the chances of reoffence.

The Act nowhere defines the meaning of the term 'superintendent or care taker'. The superintendent, under the Rules however, is a person who is required to stay in the observation home and supervise the overall care of the children or juveniles and take decisions in the case of any crisis and emergency. In case he/she is unable to stay in the home for legitimate reasons than any other senior staff member of the observation home shall stay in the institution. He is the officer-in-charge of the observation home till the release of the person from that home. He is assisted by the staff members of the home. He is entrusted to provide various facilities to the juvenile inmates during their temporal stay which includes, food, clothes, medication in case ofillness to the inmates etc. The Act does not prescribe any check on the exercise of these functions by the superintendant. On the contrary, in many cases the superintendent has been accused of committing physical and sexual abuse of the juveniles.

As a result many of the juvenile abscond from the observation homes. In one of the case action was taken against the superintendent of observation home for "willfully neglecting the victim and exposing him to physical suffering" by six senior inmates. In another incident, a minor boy was allegedly subjected to sexual harassment by a guard on duty at the government observation home in Sukher, Rajasthan, whereby notice was issued to the superintendent.

Similarly in one such incident children of the observation home at Poojappura alleged routine physical assault by the caretaker against a disabled inmate. The charges were made before a visiting team comprising of the Legislative Committee for the Welfare of Women and Children. During interaction with other inmates it was revealed that they were also subjected to caning by the caretakers on a regular basis. The committee responded by stating that action would be taken against the caretakers. But there are many such cases where the ill treatment by the caretakers or superintendents goes unreported.

The Board is expected to expeditiously dispose of an

inquiry so that the juvenile facing charge is not unnecessarily disrupted for a long period and his rehabilitation process starts at the earliest. Prolonged incarceration pending an inquiry causes trauma to the juvenile. Observation Homes, generally have no facilities for vocational training nor ways to keep juveniles occupied, thus resulting in juveniles getting restless and desperate. Due to prolonged incarceration there have been instances when juveniles have escaped or tried to escape from Observation homes, or have gone on a rampage causing destruction within the institution.

As per a study conducted under the patronage of Juvenile Justice Committee of Gauhati High Court and commissioned by the State Child Protection Society, Assam, UNICEF, "One of the key reasons for overall delays in the system is that police are not directly producing the juveniles in conflict with law before the board. It was found that it is common for the police to record the age of the juveniles as between 18 to 19 years and forward the child to a regular court, although it is clear from appearance or other sources that the accused is a juvenile". Under the Act of 2000, the age of a juvenile must be determined within 30 days, but in reality it was achieved in just 54 per cent of the cases. In some cases it took more than 90 days to determine the age of the accused. Delay in transferring the records from the courts to the boards and submitting charge sheets were identified as reasons hampering the activities. Now under the Act of 2015, the process of age determination has been amended with the provision that the age determination test shall be completed within 15 days from the date of order of the Board.

It is impossible to accurately assess the mental capacity of a child and such an assessment "exceeds the limits of science". Despite this, the Act requires the JJB to assess the mental and physical capacity of the child to commit the offence that they have been accused of. The Act provides no guidance on how to determine such capacity. The arbitrariness of these tests is further worsened by the fact that the Act does not mandate the JJB to use an expert or a psychologist for such assessment. Section 15 of the Act states that the JJB 'may' seek assistance from a psychologist or from experts. In reality, such assistance is often not sought. In the words of the Allahabad High Court, this is a "really scary state of affairs". Further, as per section 20 of the Act, when the child attains the age of twenty-one years, the Children's Court must decide whether they have "undergone reformative change" and whether they can be a "contributing member of the society".

The case of *Durga v State of Rajasthan* demonstrates the flaw in the test that is used to determine whether a child must be tried as an adult. In this case, a child had killed her husband during a fight. She was found to have the mental capacity to commit the crime because she was "cooperative and communicative" and was not in a state of excitement (three months after the incident). The JJB completely ignored the fact that her husband was an alcoholic who beat her regularly for three years and had even poured kerosene on her. To make matters worse, the JJB relied on a secret report and did not take the assistance of an expert or a psychologist.

The tests laid down in the Act are extremely vague and they do not provide any criteria to determine what 'mental capacity' and 'reformative change' constitute. Such tests are thus highly subjective and arbitrary and might allow bias to creep into the decision. The problem with such arbitrary tests is that they leave the child with a grave sense of injustice. A child who was tried as an adult or who was not considered 'reformed' upon attaining twenty-one years of age would feel like the system is not legitimate or fair, given that the tests are extremely arbitrary. Consequently, they would harbour a sense of injustice. They would also compare themself to other children who were released because they were considered 'reformed' or were not considered 'mentally capable' of committing a crime. Unless proper and convincing reasons exist to justify such differential treatment, which is unlikely given the very nature of the tests, the child's feelings of injustice would only be furthered.

It has been found empirically that a perception of injustice can increase crime and violence. There are various theories that can be used to explain this causal relationship. According to Tyler's Compliance Theory, if a citizen doesn't believe that the law is legitimate, they would not feel obligated to follow that law. It would dilute the normative values that deal with legal compliance, and hence, citizens would be less likely to abide by the law. According to the Neutralisation Theory, children find ways to neutralise their guilt and justify their actions. A sense of injustice could be one of the neutralisation techniques. They lose faith in the system and use the injustice they faced to justify their criminal behaviour.

The General Strain Theory ('GST') proposes that strain leads to negative emotions (anger and frustration), which require a coping strategy. Recent research on GST has shown that a sense of injustice is a stressor. Violence and resorting to criminal acts could be one of the possible reactions to these negative emotions. Thus, there is an empirical as well as a theoretical basis to support the claim that a sense of injustice could lead to further violence and consequently, recidivism.

It must be noted here that even if we were to revert to the older system in which juveniles were sent to remand homes only, we need to ensure that the law is implemented properly. India's observation homes have been described as 'hellholes' because of the sexual and physical abuse that children are subject to and the inhumane conditions in which they are forced to live. Further, due to a lack of infrastructure and inefficiencies in implementation (such as police subversion and the excess time taken to determine the actual age of the juvenile), many juveniles are actually lodged in prisons and subject to abuse and violence. Hence, India needs to strengthen the implementation of the law to ensure meaningful rehabilitation.

The route the justice system takes and the experience these children have, in their often barbarous journey, is an environment after which they are expected to repatriate into the society with correctional behaviours. Lack of library, vocational training, counsellors and circulation of narcotic drugs is oppugnant to the purpose of rejuvenation of young minds. Direct release from a culture that upholds violence as a tool for correctional behaviour leads to recidivism and reinforced psychological disorders which make psychological intervention imperative. As exemplified by the probation officers' dismissive attitude, lack of understanding of the origins of their criminality is the root cause of the detrimental turnabout of juveniles' behaviour. These patterns of violation and anomaly of the JJ Act can be attributed to four factors: flimsy infrastructural support in the form of economic and human resources, inefficient selection criteria for supervisors, sociocultural tendencies that lean towards political corruption, physical exploitation of children, and a total sense of ambiguity over who is responsible for upholding the system.

There are anomalies antithetical to the aim. And the juvenile homes have become homes where inmates, who are kids below 18 years of age, are subjected to sexual assault on different levels. These kids are however, forced to live in inhuman conditions are treated very badly in these so-called shelter/ correction homes. Also, there is no authorized location for these juvenile homes and are situated anywhere across India, be it a small town or the national capital. n a report that was prepared by Asian Centre for Human Rights (ACHR) reports cases of systematic and often repeated sexual assault on children in juvenile justice homes. The reports say out of the total 39 cases, 11 cases were reported from government-run juvenile justice homes. These government homes comprise of observation homes, children homes, shelter homes and orphanages. One case a CWC member was accused of sexual harassment during counselling sessions. The remaining 27 cases were reported from privately/NGO run juvenile justice homes such as shelter homes, orphanages, children homes, destitute homes, etc. Majority of privately/ NGO run homes are not registered under Section 34(3) of the Juvenile Justice (Care and Protection of Children) Act, 2006, as per reports by *India Times.*

As per reports by *India Times,* government run Ashiana Home for Boys at Alipur in Delhi, a 12-year-old HIV positive boy was allegedly sexually abused in the national capital by a security guard and other older inmates. An incident that occurred in Suparna Ka Aangan in Gurgaon, Haryana saw similar incidences where the owner, identified as Suparna Sethi and 20-year old caretaker Rachit Raju of the NGO allegedly raped minor girl inmate. Both of them were arrested for violation of the Juvenile Justice (Care and Protection of Children) Act, 2000 as the orphanage was not registered and sent to judicial custody.

Another shocking incident from Haryana was reported where a girl inmate of the government-run shelter home Bal Kunj at Yamunanagar, went missing. As per reports, the juveniles in the shelter homes were subjected to sexual and mental harassment by the caretakers and the owners. Due to a rise in such incidences, the state government ordered a probe by the Haryana State Council for Child Welfare (HSCCW) into the allegation of sexual abuse of the inmates of the shelter home.

The police are the first point of contact for most children before they step into child care institutions. Each district of the country is mandated to have a Special Juvenile Police Unit (SJPU) – a body of police officers that are specifically trained in child rights – who must file initial cases and bring children forward to their first committee hearing within 24 hours. While most states do not even have the requisite SJPU outlined by the law, the vast majority of SJPU's are poorly trained and remain ignorant of the JJA.

This preliminary interaction sets the tone for what India's most vulnerable children are to expect for the remainder of their time in government custody. It is not unusual to hear cases of physical abuse and mistreatment at the police station, even before their official registration within the system. While it is specifically mentioned that "In no case shall a juvenile in conflict with law be placed in a police lockup or lodged in a jail," the police scarcely adhere to this rule. A study of observation homes and special homes across Maharashtra found that amongst the CICL who had been interviewed, 65 percent were kept in the lock-up ranging for a timespan of 2–13 days. While the study also found that the police behaved affectionately with CNCP, often offering them food or spending money from their own pockets, CICL were treated abusively. Sixty-seven percent of CICL had reportedly been slapped, 30 percent were beaten severely, 32 percent had been whipped with a belt, 15 percent had been hung from the ceiling, and 1.7 percent had been sexually abused. Qualitative evidence has revealed multiple case studies where children have been restrained in jails, underfed, or beaten into confessions, predominantly affecting boys from underprivileged backgrounds. Many children refrain from speaking out on these experiences because they have been threatened by the police into silence.

As far as the causes for such maltreatment go, state governments are perfectly aware of this widespread phenomena and argue that this is the result of "inadequate training," a "lack of clarity on determination of age among police officers for children in conflict with law," "no fit facility to house CNPC and CICL between sunset and sunrise," and a "reluctance to release CICL on bail due to social pressure from victim's kin, media, etc". While many of their excuses are grounded in infrastructural limitations or widespread demands for retributive justice over rehabilitative justice (following the infamous 2012 gang-rape case involving underage offenders), it is important to note the cultural dimensions of this problem and the historical acceptance and normalization of violence against children across India.

For generations, the physical and psychological abuse of children has been permissible by cultural beliefs and purported economic constraints, such as "the need for child marriage" or superstitions that "sex with a young virgin" can cure sexually transmitted diseases. Acts of violence like slapping or the twisting of ears are routine, and children are often expected to engage in laborious activities from a young age to contribute towards the family income. A quick glance at international statistics shows that "India has the world's largest number of sexually abused children, with a child below 16 years raped every 155th minute, a child below 10 every 13th hour, and one in every 10 children sexually abused at any point in time. India also has the largest number of missing children". These social and cultural patterns invariably translate into the weak implementation of safety standards for children within the system. Moreover, the socialization of communities into a culture that upholds violence as a natural tool to control behaviors provides little incentive for children or their families to report these violations of their human rights – much less to view them as such.

Children are frequently misallocated, resulting in uncomfortable groupings of victims and offenders across all ages and genders. Once children have been placed in government custody, their direct channel of communication with their adjudicating committees and their families are Probation Officers (POs). Essentially their personalized caseworkers, POs are staff-members of the juvenile justice home, entrusted with attending to all the physical and socioemotional needs of the child. POs learn and record each child's personal history, provide avenues for education and play, and importantly, they follow up with the child *after* their release from the institution.

Unfortunately, as is consistent with the larger failures of the system, this is not the reality of what POs actually do. Given the national and state-wide restrictions on funding, there simply is not enough capacity for POs to allocate the care and attention needed to learn about each child or to follow up with them after their release. A considerable challenge within this landscape is the reality that India is a geographically massive country, with an equally massive population to protect under the system. With a minimum requirement of *one* observation home per district (which is a gigantic entity, sometimes covering 11 million people) juvenile justice homes face the risk of being overcrowded, understaffed, and too under-resourced to provide even basic resources like food, bedding, or a change of clothes. In the case of Maharashtra, for example, the child-to-PO ratio is 139:1, while the legally prescribed ratio is 33:1.

Ms. Suparna Gupta – the founder and director of Aangan, an NGO that works to reform over six hundred juvenile justice homes across the country – argues that this lack of funding has created a vicious cycle of vulnerability for children. "When there are mass raids in factories by NGOs like *Pratham*, they bring about 100 kids back to the home, and they will just be parked there because there is no place for them — not even to stretch your legs and sleep. So there are all these exhausted children, and then there is the pressure to say, 'look at their health, let's quickly send them home', and they get sent back into this cycle of being trafficked. In a lot of districts, one home is just not enough." While family reunification is generally the most desired outcome, this can be an extremely dangerous option without a thorough home assessment. A recent study that examines the child-trafficking pathway from Bihar to Rajasthan found that the infrastructural problems within the juvenile justice system have exacerbated the potential for children to be re-trafficked. By surveying various POs across multiple districts in Bihar, they found "hugely divergent responses as to whether a home verification report is conducted," and that "respondents stated that thorough assessments of the potential risks and suitability of a family environment 'do not physically happen". The fact that most children come from low-income, rural, or migrant families presents a particular challenge for POs to ascertain their family situations within their limited budgets. Given a lack of home assessments, coupled with growing pressure for deinstitutionalization, children are acutely vulnerable to being exploited.

The severe underestimation of what it costs to protect India's children has forced the government to cut corners where they can, leaving POs with little support on the ground. They have dissolved important job vacancies within child care institutions and have been filling vacant positions with underpaid contractual workers.

Finally, similar to the selection process of committee

members, the manner in which POs are appointed breeds a systematic indifference towards the protection of child rights. Aangan's mixed-methods study on POs across Maharashtra found that there was no formal process by which they were entrusted with this job. More than half of the POs surveyed had not even applied for the position but were arbitrarily transferred to fill vacancies within the district. As a result, they had little to no expertise in counseling, mentoring, or evaluating the socio-psychological needs of children.

Given the unpredictable nature of their appointments, POs scarcely receive training to prepare for the immense amount of responsibilities that are thrust upon them. A PO working in an NGO-run institution for the last decade said that in all his years on the job, "I have never attended any training for any subject...we learn on the job". As a consequence, there is a general sense of ignorance towards child rights and overwhelmingly negative assumptions about the need for rehabilitation. When asked about how they counsel the children in their custody, some PO's responded that "counseling will not make a difference if they are repeat offenders" — touting the exact retributivist sentiments that the JJA sought to dismantle.

References

1. National Human Rights Commission. (2004). Minor raped in a Juvenile Home at Hyderabad gets relief.

2. Department for Women, Children, Disabled and Senior Citizens. (2016). *Audit Report on 'General & Social Sector' for the year 2015, Chapter III Compliance Audit Observations.*

3. Ceremila A. (2020). Orphans and juvenile criminals share accommodation in Warangal. *Deccan Herald.*

4. Ceremila A. (2021). Government Children's home goes out of reach in Warangal. Orphans and juvenile criminals share accommodation in Warangal. *Deccan Herald.*

5. Bhoge, N. D., Panse, S. N., Pawar, A. V., Raparti, G. T., Ramanand, S. J., & Ramanand, J.B. (2017). Study of sociodemographic profile of juvenile boys admitted in an observation home. *International Journal of Advances in Medicine*, *4*(1), 230-237.

6. Reddy P. (2020). Security lapses suspected at observation home in Warangal. Telangana today.

7. (2018). Fifteen boys escape from juvenile home. The Times of India.

8. Sudhir U. (2015). Critics Slam Jail-Like Atmosphere After Death of 11-Year-Old in Hyderabad Juvenile Home. NDTV India.

9. National Commission for Protection of Child Rights (2019). *NCPCR Report: India, Key Findings at a Glance.*

10. Delhi High Court Juvenile Justice Committee. (2006). *Brief note on constitution and functioning of juvenile justice committee.*

Conclusion

The plight of children in observation homes was accentuated in the national audit of the CCIs by the National Commission for the Protection of Child Rights. Lok Sabha passed the JJ Bill 2021 introduced by the Minister of Women and Child Development, which amends provisions regarding CCLs and CNCPs. However, the bill fails to stipulate requisite amendments for coherent functioning of OHs and norms for better protection of children.

Increasing the number of probationary officers, counselors, follow-up programs and segregation of juveniles is indispensable. The OHs require immediate infrastructural renovation to remove any resemblance to lockups or jails and inclusion of more dormitories in consonance with the need for segregation, adequate toilets, and bathrooms, dining hall, and kitchen. There must be a strict prohibition placed on engaging CCLs for cleaning the washrooms, dormitories or any part of the OH and workers must be availed for this purpose. Each OH should be equipped with adequate amenities such as mattresses, pillows, blankets footwear, and separate toiletries for each child. Quality of Food and water should be never compromised ensuring maximum nutrition quotient, followed by regular inspection of the food storage room and maintenance of the health record of each child throughout his stay in the OH. Health checkups every fortnight and a separate hygienic sick room equipped with a first aid kit are necessary. After providing due training, requisite staff including counselors, teachers, and nurses should be appointed to ensure individual attention to children in conflict with the law. A robust mechanism of immediate inquiry and requisite disciplinary action should be ensured against any manhandling or violation by the staff. Education, vocational training, and counseling should be tailored according to the demographics (crime mapping) and educational qualifications of each child, and records w.r.tclasses conducted, books provided and the courses taught should be duly maintained.

The Individual Care Plans are to be made for every CCL by the Probation Officer within 2 days of joining with updates every consecutive day, with a separate record of parental visits, JJB members' visits, Inspection Committee visits, and for medical records. Suggestion box and a robust grievance redressal system are the immediate need of the hour and Information regarding the Childline services, District Legal Services Authority, JJB members must be displayed in the OH for easy access to children and parents. Stringent security including trained security guards verified by police, liaising with the local police for emergencies, and elevated walls with barbed fencing with CCTVs is indispensable. Direct admonition, release, or stigmatized semantics can lead to recidivism and reinforced psychological disorders which make psychological intervention imperative. A child-friendly rehabilitator environment with requisite integration of parents in the process is mandatory, or else there will always be lacunae in the process of implementation of the JJ Act. Providing employment opportunities post-release of the child is advisory to prevent recidivism and eliminate the need for resorting to criminal activities due to impoverishment.

The juvenile justice system entails a robust mechanism of therapeutic intervention for rehabilitation for prevention recidivism among miscreants. The legislature recognises the lack of potential in juveniles for requisite mens rea, and the need to observe and rehabilitate these miscreants who lack the capability to comprehend the consequences of their conduct. However, the reality of observation homes in Telangana are far from the prospect, where after months of lockup, unhygienic conditions, inhumane behaviour, and under nutrition, children are expected to repatriate into the society with correctional behaviours. Such treacherous environment with amalgamation of CNCPs with the CCLs will lead to oppugnant results envisioning a despairing state of society. The route the justice system takes and the experience these children have in their often barbarous journey through the justice system may coarse the developing minds, anddwarfing of intellect. The solution does not explicitly lie in the new bill of 2021, but the stricter provisions regarding qualification of CWC and power of scrutiny on District Magistrate may filter the baneful influences on young minds.

Viewing the system in its entirety, we see that the mistreatment of children across juvenile justice homes has been an ongoing, permitted phenomena due to four factors: flimsy infrastructural support in the form of economic and human resources, inefficient selection criteria for jobs that are immensely important, sociocultural tendencies that lean towards political corruption and the physical exploitation of children, and a total sense of ambiguity over who is responsible for upholding the system. All these push factors — and a long list of others too intricate and disheartening to mention in this article — intersect with each other to create the amalgamation of buildings, committees, and individuals that have brought immense harm upon approximately 40 million children within the system.

What's most unsettling about this failure in public policy (and failure in human rights) is the sheer quantity of children that are being implicated from impoverished, lower-caste, and Muslim communities. Considering the main demographics that are vulnerable to entering juvenile justice homes reveals how the system ultimately institutionalizes neglect and oppression of *specific subgroups* of Indian society — those that have been pushed to the fringes of political participation, social equality, and economic opportunity for as long as their communities can remember. The government has essentially created a reinforcing mechanism for socio-economic deprivation where children of marginalized communities enter the system, experience abuse, and face increasing risks of remaining marginalized after their eventual release from these homes. This demographic salience has also meant that political elites have been lukewarm at best towards seizing the issue and pushing the conversation as a national priority. Any public outrage after media exposure of specific sexual assault cases in childshelters has been sporadic and passing, perhaps even fueling the impression of systemic change without any meaningful political action. A 2007 study found that "In the last four years, on an average, only 2.7 percent of the questions asked in Parliament by members related to children" and that "60 percent of these questions were on education".

It follows, then, that raising widespread public awareness about this issue is a critical solution that might garner more political support for a costly systemic overhaul. As Enakshi Ganguly insightfully noted, "Today, we are not doing social policy based on the principles of non-discrimination and enhancing dignity anymore. Because social change is also measured in the same way that corporate change is measured, we see that investments in social policy will never yield immediate returns. That's how we're in this mess — nobody has the patience to really build the system ground-up" [Beyond just articles in the media – which only target a small segment of India's literate (and typically elite) population – public information campaigns that inspire a sense of outrage among the communities most affected are vital to change. Films, TV shows, and school curricula could start including figures on the magnitude of this crisis, using anonymized case-studies about the experiences of children within the system. NGOs could collaborate with popular public figures who are widely known and viewed by all demographics of Indians, thereby generating political support through their endorsements. The Indian government has historically capitalized on the general illiteracy and ignorance of its citizens as a means to uphold the status quo, which is why a strong public policy solution must also break this cycle.

Other policy fixes include changes in selection procedures for many of these stakeholders who have been given enormous responsibilities over the lives of children. Disallowing states from picking their political supporters and mandating that positions of members on inspection committees, CWCs, and JJBs be fulltime positions would be fruitful, easy fixes that might encourage more oversight and professionalism within the system. But given that much of the institutional corruption can be attributed to sociocultural tendencies, all of these policies have to be implemented in tandem with long-term sociological solutions.

For example, our cultural perception of these children has not yet aligned with the facts of what brought them into the system to begin with. As exemplified by the probation officers' dismissive attitudes towards providing counselling, treatment of children across the country is still largely determined by the lack of understanding of the origins of their criminality. Studies on children's homes found that 10 percent have never been to school and 72.5 percent had already begun full-time work at the age of 14. In fact, the vast majority of these children are contributing as much as 40 percent of their family's income before being apprehended. This data reveals how children in India are prematurely thrust into adulthood, and thereby exposed to a plethora of vulnerabilities that place them in the system to begin with. "If you push young people into adulthood so early, they will behave like adults *sans* the cognitive ability to, and with whatever role models of adulthood around them," says Ms. Ganguly, who has been advocating for a radical shift in our discourse on juvenile delinquents. She argues that "We are creating these terrible circumstances and then punishing them for it violently." A robust training program for police officers and probation officers on child rights (whilst transparently sharing data on the causes for their criminality) might be an effective way to kick-start these cultural shifts.

Finally, from an equity standpoint, one of the most important solutions might be simply to seek continuous feedback from the children within the system. By mandating a monthly feedback process, where children can freely speak their minds, we could simultaneously learn about their experiences of abuse, their individual contexts that brought them into the system, and possible solutions to keep them safe.

We can say that juveniles who are involved in the crime are not criminals, in fact, they are victims of society. The Supreme Court, while hearing the cases related to juvenile delinquency observed that for a crime like rape and murder, it is hard to conceive that the juvenile is not aware of the consequences. For instance, a boy of seventeen years of age has killed the father of another boy of seventeen years of age, then whose rights are we talking about, a perpetrator or the victim. It is clear that the victim has the right to "Right to Justice". No doubt, the present legislature has the provision for those juvenile aged 16-18 years and having committed a heinous crime may be tried as an adult. But the final decision to consider a juvenile aged 16-18 years as an adult depends on the juvenile justice board and the children's court. The parameters on which juvenile justice board and children's court take a decision are not well-defined in the legislation. A case in point is Khan vs State of Maharashtra. Another area of concern is the high pendency of cases before the juvenile justice board. As per the data available, at the end of 2018, around 41709 were pending with juveniles justice board. Hence, we are over legislated but under enforced country as far as Juvenile Justice is concerned. Another issue in juvenile crime is most of the cases are from substance abuse. A majority of them are between the ages of 15 and 18, belonging to lower socio-economic classes, and are dropouts from schools. The most commonly used narcotics are alcohol, heroin, cannabis and inhalants. Peer pressure is the most common cause of indulging into drugs. Nearly half of the boys began taking drugs when they were between the ages of 10 and 14, and more than half were involved in anti-social activities to meet drug expenses. Many psychologists now feel that the children are grown-ups by the age of 14 years, and are responsible for their actions. Besides, in the last few decades, the maturity level of child has increased significantly and now a 16 year old juvenile can easily comprehend their actions and its consequences. It means there is an advancement of maturity among the children today. Also, if we look at NCRB data, around 56,031 boys aged between 16-18 years were convicted for crime under IPC and SLL whereas conviction rate for girls between the same age group was only 333. So, on the basis of above data, one of the reforms required in the current law can be reducing boy's juvenility age to 16 years. Also, the parameters on the basis of which juvenile justice board decides, whether the juvenile can be treated as an adult or not, need to more crystallized. This will ensure more objectivity in the working of juvenile justice board.

The problem of juvenile delinquency is not of recent origin. It existed in societies through the ancient times. Rather it has become a global problem. To redress the issue of juvenile delinquency various declarations and conventions at the international level and laws were enacted by the respective governments at the national level. With the passage of time and advancement of information technology existing juvenile laws were proved to be ineffective to curb the rising incidents of juvenile crimes.

Index

a new concept of juvenile justice 114
"a youthful offender" 58
Abuzar Hossain v. State of West Bengal 100
Administration of Juvenile Justice, 1985 85
adult crime and juvenile delinquency 47
adult criminal justice system 83
"adversary combative proceedings" 72
"Age Memo" 83
Aggressive behavior 39
ancient Hindu codes 48
ancient Indian legal system 49
Antisocial youth 41
Apex Court 61
Apprentices Act of 1850 56
Arnit Das v. State of Bihar 28
"Arrest Memo" 83
Article 12 (2) 125
Article 14
---------- in breach of 31 30, 85
Article 14(3)(b) 90
Article 14(3)(d) 90
Article 14(4) 99
Article 14.2 104
Article 15 (3) 10
Article 15(3) 81
Article 19(1) 110
Article 20(1) 91
Article 20(3) 87
Article 21 82, 101
Article 21-A 102
Article 21A 82

Article 22(1) 18, 89
Article 22(2) 93, 94
Article 226 82
Article 253 84
Article 350-A 102
Article 37(a) 109
Article 39 (e) and (f) 81
Article 39-A 18, 89
Article 40(1) 18
Article 40(2)(a) 92
Article 40(2)(b)(i) 97
Article 40(2)(b)(ii) 95
Article 40(2)(b)(iv) 107
Article 40(3) 98, 99
Article40(2)(b)(ii) 87
Articles 23 and 24 81
Articles 37 and 38 33
Ashiana Home 184
Ashu Kumar v. State of Uttar Pradesh 96
Asian Centre for Human Rights 176, 184

Bail as a matter of right 95
Bal Kunj 184
basic juvenile justice philosophy 71
battle of Buxsur 48
battle of Plassay 48
Bengal Children Act, 1922 61
"best interests" 19
biological age 25
Bombay Children Act 1924 61

Capaldi and Patterson 42
care and deprived of liberty 13
CCIs 12
CEDAW 84
Census of India 22
Child Protection Policy 165
Child rape 176
Child Welfare Police Officer 104
Child-friendly procedures 105, 106
children in CCI 13
Children in Conflict with the Law 10
Children in Need of Care and Protection 10
Code of Conduct 139
Code of Hammurabi 16, 49
commit serious crimes 45
committed crimes 169
Community variations 44
Community-based statistics 44
Complaint and redressal mechanism 141
crime and delinquency 47
crimes against children 9
criminal and criminality 73

criminal justice system 7, 31, 70, 74
Criminal Law 22
Criminal Procedure Code 1861 56
criminal trial 72, 73
Criminal Tribes Amendment Act, 1897 58
criminogenic culture 36
custodial interrogation 105
custody in CCIs 13

DCPU 90
death penalty or life imprisonment 112
Delhi gang-rape case 85
"delinquent children" 47
Delinquent juveniles 28
Deprivation of liberty 129, 146
discourse on juvenile delinquents 196
DLSA 90
Doli Incapax 24, 28, 29
Dr. Hira Singh 67
Dr. Subramanian Swamy 30
Durga v State of Rajasthan 181

Early Chinese Law 49
Enakshi Ganguly 194
English legal system 48, 49
Evidence Act 106

Family Influences 41
Family Interaction 43
Family Structure 41
Free legal aid 23, 150
"fundamental principle" 97

gang-rape case 186
General Strain Theory 182
German Law 51
"get away" 65

Haryana State Council for Child Welfare 185
'hellholes' 183
Hindu and Muslim customary laws 48
Hindu ethical codes 48
Humanitarian and religious features 47

Inder Singh v. Delhi Admn. 62
Indian judicial system 49
Indian justice system 29
Indian Penal Code 1860 22, 56
Individual Child Care Plan 133
Information about charges 94
Institution of Probation system 61
Integrated Child Protection Scheme (ICPS) guideline 133

International Covenant on Civil and Political Right 84
International Platform 76

Jail Committee's Repor 61
JJ Act, 2000 93, 98
JJ Act, 2015 14, 18, 19, 76, 82, 85, 89, 98, 104, 168
JJ Bill 2021 191
JJ Model Rules, 2016 14, 89, 102, 106
JJ Rules (2016) 132
JJB proceedings 171
JJB within 24 hours 94
Justice 65, 66
Justice J.S. Verma 32
juvenile court cases 43
juvenile crime 197
juvenile delinquency 35, 36
----------- The problem of 35
juvenile delinquency or child offenders 48
juvenile justice
----- most significant feature of the 70
------------ The case of 63
Juvenile Justice (Care and Protection Act, 2015 7, 12, 13, 14, 17, 20, 26
Juvenile Justice Act 28, 32, 177
Juvenile Justice Act, 1960 23
Juvenile Justice Act, 2000 30
Juvenile Justice Act,1986 115
Juvenile Justice Board 11, 34, 176, 197
juvenile justice delivery system 60
juvenile justice mechanism 25
Juvenile Justice System 12, 17, 59, 64, 65, 66, 69, 70, 71, 73, 86, 120, 121, 125, 129, 130, 193
----------- in India 7, 8, 10, 11, 18, 59
juvenile police Bureau 67
juvenile under twelve years 51
Juvenile Welfare Board 115
Juvenility predominantly 25

Kautilya 48

Labeo and Ulpianus 50
Life Skill Education 136

Madras Children Act, 1920 61
Manu 48
"mark sheet" 28
medieval German Law 51
'mental capacity' 181
Mental health 149
'mentally capable' 182
Model Prison Manual 12

Ms Ganguly 174, 196
Ms. Kiran Bedi 32
Ms. Suparna Gupta 187
Muslim religious philosophy 49
mysterious circumstances 174

Narcotic Drugs and Psychotropic Substances Act, 19 96
National Commission for Protection of Child Rights 176, 177
National Crime Records Bureau 9
National Human Rights Commission 105
National Skill Development Programme 158
"Nirbhaya" case 33
Non-retroactive juvenile justice 91

Observation Home or Special Home 104
operative fragmentary variables of juvenile justic 59

Paramedical and Psychologist 137
"parens patrae" philosophy 67
peer delinquent behavior 45
Peer Influences 45
physical and sexual abuse 179
Physical Health 149
physical punishments 44
physically or sexually abused 174
'pilla jail' 177
Place of Safety 11, 159, 163, 164, 165
plea of juvenility 100
POCSO Act 111
----------- 2012 98, 99, 110
post-sentence juvenile justice 58
Pratham 188
Pre-Roman and Greek Law 49
Prenatal and Perinatal
---------- complications" 38
---------- Factors 38
---------- risk factors 38
Presumption of Innocence 97
prevention of crime 10
Prevention of Juvenile Delinquency, 1990 85
Principle of dignity and worth 124
Principle of equality and non-discrimination 128
Principle of family responsibility 126

Principle of non-stigmatizing semantics 127
Principle of non-waiver of rights 127
Principle of right to privacy and confidentiality 128
Principles of natural justice 130
problem-solving processing patterns 41
Procedural safeguards 93
Prof. Ved Kumari 79
Professor Colin Howard 29
Prohibition against imposition of death penalty 112
Prosocial behaviors 40
Protection from torture and ill-treatment 109
Protection norms and emergency 138
Protection of Children from Sexual Offences Act, 2 96
protective custody 134
Public Utility Litigation provisions 23

"qualified immunity" 24

Rachit Raju 184
rapid changes 35
Ravi-ul-Islam v. State 96
re-enactment of juvenile justice legislation 76
'reformative change' 181
"reformative philosophy" 57
Reformatory School Act of 1854 and 1855 52
Reformatory School in 1899 53
Reformatory Schools Act, 1876 16, 53
Reformatory Schools Act of 1897 57, 58
registration of Child Care Institutions 163
Report of the Indian Jails Committee 59
Report of the Indian Jails Committee, 1919-20 122
Restorative justice 167
---------- practices 169
Right of Children to Free and Compulsory Education 103
Right to be dealt 99
Right to be heard 106
Right to be Protected from Sexual Offences 110
Right to child 104
--------- friendly procedures 104
Right to Education 102
------------ and Non-Discrimination 85
Right to fair and speedy inquiry 101

"Right to Justice" 196
Right to life 101
Right to Privacy 108
Right to rehabilitative dispositions 111
Rise in juvenile delinquencies 16
risk of juvenile delinquency 40
Roman Law(Twelve Tables) 50
Rule 10(5) 95
Rule 7.1 88
Rule 8(3)(iii) 88
Rule 87(d) 110
Rules 8(3)(i) 93, 94
Rules 8(3)(i) and 9(1) 94

Safety and Security 150
Salil Bali v. Union of India 86
Sampurna Behura v. Union of India 83
scientific method of investigation 72
Section 1(4)(i) 98
Section 10(1) 93, 94
Section 15 181
Section 18(2) 104
Section 19(1)(i) 101
Section 2(13) 91, 92
Section 2(21) 20
Section 2(9) 19
Section 24(1) 86
Section 29-B 57
Section 3 19
Section 3(i) 97
Section 3(iii) 108
Section 34(1) 99
Section 5 92
Section 5, JJ Act, 2015 91
Section 562 57
Section 75(1) 109
Sections 29-B 57
Sections 82 and 83 30
Segregation 135
seventh Five Year Plan 121
sexual abuse 174
sexual and mental harassment 184
Sexual assault 175
Sexual Offences 110
sexually transmitted diseases 176
Sheela Barse v Union of India, 1986 122
Sheela Barse v. Union of India 82
SLSA 90
Social Setting 44
socio-economic conditions 42
Special Juvenile Police Unit 185
special laws and policies 10

Standards of care 164
Studies of criminal activity 37
Suparna Ka Aangan 184
Suparna Sethi 184

Talwinder Singh v. State of Punjab 96
Tappan 70
The Beijing Rules 77, 78
the case of juvenile justice 63
the Children Act,1960 120
the Code of Criminal Procedure, 1973 96
The concept of juvenile court 53
The Delhi High Court Juvenile Justice Committee 123
The Doctrine of Doli Incapax 24
The essence of the Juvenile Justice 86
The essence of the Juvenile Justice (Care and Prot 86
the formal system of juvenile justice 68
the handling of juvenile offenders 47
The Havana Rules 77, 78
the history of juvenile justice 58
The Indian Penal Code 57
The Individual Care Plans 192
The Industrial School Act 53
The JJ Act, 2015 109, 111
The JJ Model Rules, 2016 106, 111
The Juvenile Justice 85
The Juvenile Justice (Care and Protection of Child) 11
The Juvenile Justice (Care and Protection) Act 19
The Juvenile Justice Act 123
The Juvenile Justice Act, 1986 83, 115, 120, 144
The Juvenile Justice Board 131
The Juvenile Justice System 16
The juvenility based Doli incapax 30
The Legal Services Authorities Act, 1987 18
The Matsya Purana 48
the Mosaic Code 49
the nature of juvenile delinquency 7
The POCSO Act, 2012 110, 111
The presumption of Doli Incapax 29
The problem of juvenile delinquency 198
The RTE Act 103
Therapeutic jurisprudence 16
therapy sessions 153
torture and ill-treatment 109
Transfer, Release and After Care 153

treatment and socialization of juvenile offenders 58
treatment for juvenile delinquents 16
'trouble makers' 13
Twelve Tables 50
Tyler's Compliance Theory 182

U.P. Children Act, 1951 28
UN Convention on the Rights of the Child, 1989 18
UNCRC 13, 79, 84
---------- Committee 125
UNCRPD) 84
"undergone reformative change" 181
UNICEF 180
United Nations Standard Minimum Rules 19, 76, 83
Unplanned Urbanization 36

"variety of disposition orders" 77
Verma Committee Report 33
Vishaka v. State of Rajasthan 84

Yajanavalkya 48
"young criminals" 47